BRIDGE STUDENT SUCCESS

EFFORT + STRENGTHS + CRITICAL THINKING + COOPERATION

An Education 2 Aspire
Toolbox for Academic Success

DAVID T. JONES

Cover and interior illustrations by Kevin Cannon
ISBN 13: 978-1-64343-553-4
Library of Congress Catalog Number: 2024944542
Printed in the United States of America
First Printing: 2025
28 27 26 25 24   5 4 3 2 1

Beaver's Pond Press
939 West Seventh Street
St. Paul, MN 55102
www.BeaversPondPress.com
To order, visit www.Education2Aspire.com.

Dedication

To my loving grandparents, and my dear uncles and aunts who supported my sports endeavors and learning process.

To my dear parents, Richard Guy Jones and Ella Jean (Hout) Jones, for the caring and the inspiration, and for the belief that being independent is a very good thing. You taught me it's OK to take a risk and gain knowledge from that risk.

To my PIL, **Partner in Life**, Jo Jo Peterson, for her loving-kindness and support as I grow in my understanding of life. You're a great joy to learn from and be with as we move through life's wonderment.

To the Duluth Morgan Park community and the Goodfellow club for all the joy and support.

I am very grateful that the universe allowed me the genetics and opportunity to gain as much knowledge as possible through my mistakes and new understandings.

Praise for the Education2Aspire Approach

Mr. Jones has the experience and commitment to rethink how we support teachers. He has both classroom experience and a system-level perspective, which is critical to the success of rethinking teacher professional development. He always takes initiative and is dedicated to improving student outcomes.

—**Elise Maxwell,** former Coordinator of Human Capital,
Minneapolis Public Schools

After implementing the principles of your class for the past four months, I see my students demonstrating a more positive school attitude and improved persistence in all academic areas, including subjects that may be more challenging for them.

—**Debra Krawetz**, Middle Grades Language Arts and Social Studies Teacher,
Lake Harriet Upper School, Minneapolis Public Schools

I really enjoyed your class. There are a lot of strategies and fun ways to help students to be successful. Most of these ideas, strategies, and resources that I've gotten from the class can be used in my classroom right away.

—**Jerry Yang**, Reserve Teacher,
Hmong International Academy, Minneapolis Public Schools

Mr. Jones is one of the most upbeat professionals I've had the privilege to encounter in some time. At a time when teachers are generally feeling the nervous fatigue of negative appraisal, Mr. Jones reflects a caring, positive, effervescent enthusiasm for his job that is generally uplifting to all those he interacts with professionally.

—**Robert J. Lariccia**, Principal
Warrensville Heights Junior High, Warrensville Heights, Ohio

Foreword

As I reflect on my years as an elementary school principal, walking into Mr. Jones's classroom was an inspiration. The class was always busy, with small groups talking and working together. But where was Mr. Jones? He was walking around from one group to another, asking questions and encouraging groups. The class was happy, on task, and confident.

Change of any significance requires new knowledge, skills, and ways of doing things. David Jones has successfully incorporated important critical teaching strategies: cooperative learning, individual learning styles, and conflict resolution strategies.

Mr. Jones believes that students are a crucial part of their own learning. Observing his classroom and his interactions with students, it is evident his students have a sense of belonging and ownership in their own learning. Education2Aspire gives teachers research-backed ideas to make learning a positive experience for all children. Traditional "teacher talks/students listen" is out! Let's teach and have fun.

Donna Amann
Principal at Pillsbury Elementary

Dear David,

I am writing a letter of appreciation to you let you know how much I am grateful for your **Education2Aspire** course that I participated in last summer at the Davis Center. The research based ideas and activities that you taught us about how to inspire students to excel academically have drastically changed and improved how I approach my role as a middle school advisory teacher. Your teaching philosophy and engaging learning games based on the "growth mindset theory" that school success can be developed through dedication and hard work, have helped me to nurture my students' effort and as a result bolster their motivation and achievement.

A few examples of how I implement your course into my advisory class include instituting a weekly circle of respect discussion to talk about topics related to school success, writing in our Aspirations Journals on topics such as, "What kind of smart are you?" and filling out a weekly accountability and effort rating form.

Thank you for teaching me how to support my seventh grade advisory better. After implementing the principles of your class for the past four months, I see my students demonstrating a more positive school attitude and improved persistence in all academic areas, including the subjects that may be more challenging for them. I look forward to continuing the ideas and methods of **Education2Aspire** at Lake Harriet Upper for the remainder of the school year.

Sincerely yours,

Debra Krawetz

Debra Krawetz
Middle Grades Language Arts and
Social Studies Teacher
Lake Harriet Upper Campus

See pages 140 to 151 for examples of the Student-Effort Journal and how to implement Education2Aspire principles in advisory classroom settings.

Contents

Dear Mr. Jones, your an awesome
Teacher because you compare learning
to life or fun stuff. Also, you care about us,
listen to us, Tell Jokes to us, you make us
think outside the box. You are the
best teacher ever.

Sincerly
wilson

Dear, Mr. Jones
you're a fun 5th grade Teacher You
Made learning fun and Made an imprint
on the way I look at My life, like How
When I Roll My eyes you look at it Positive
instead of the Negitive energy I intended
I Really Apreciate you, you're the Best
teacher ever we will Not ever forget you

Sincerely
Your Best student
Hello Kitty ♥ or
Anna

Dear Mr. Jones,

Thanks for all your help
this year. we've done alot of
fun things. 5th grade is
My favorite year ever!

I like it when you say "I'm
Not mad at you, I'm mad
at your choice."

Hope you have
a great life.
Sincerely, Noah.C

Dear Mr. Jones,

This was and is the best year of my life so far.
I will remember it, will you? I loved a lot of the
things you did (Maybe not singing) I love your Jones
especialy Jim and Jon. you are the best teacher.
I loved this year. See you later.

TYL!

TTYL!

LOLZ! Remember me,
GRACE ROUE

LOLZ!

Thanks For all you did! ?

Mr. Jones

Dear. Mr. Jones, You are the Best
Teacher, Because you care about how much
We learn. You are a Sensational teacher.
I will miss you so much you made my last
year here and your last year here great. ☺
Your flabergasted student.
Samantha M.

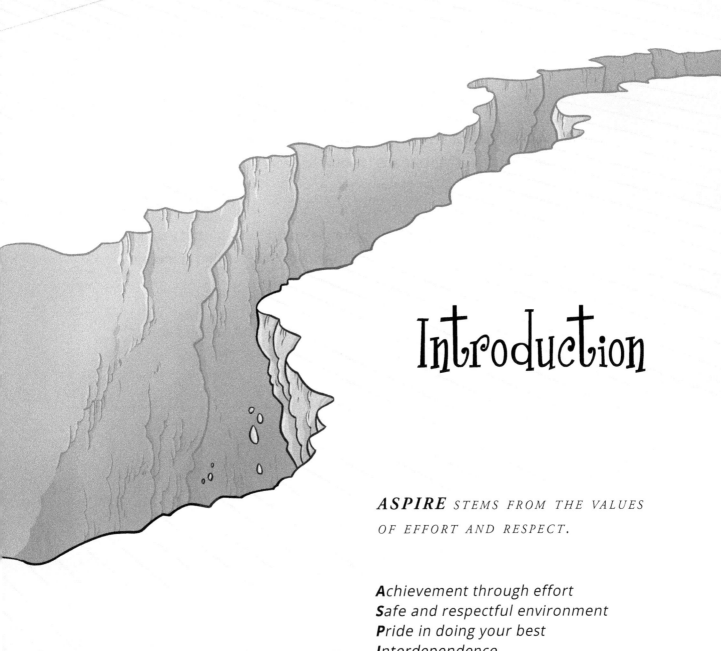

Introduction

ASPIRE *STEMS FROM THE VALUES OF EFFORT AND RESPECT.*

Achievement through effort
Safe and respectful environment
Pride in doing your best
Interdependence
Responsibility for learning
Emotional well-being

Education2Aspire is my philosophy that you, the student, can self-actualize academically, socially, and emotionally through an effort-based learning process. You will assess, monitor, and support your own learning. My belief is that you will and can create an intrinsic desire to learn and not have the external force of the adults and the rewards drive your learning.

In this book, I'll describe strategies, provide philosophical explanations, and offer hands-on illustrations for how to become the learner you deserve to be.

You will discuss your thoughts with your class and teacher, or if you are doing this book for your own self-improvement, you will find someone to discuss your thoughts with.

You deserve a joyful, successful, interesting life and career. I am committed to that belief!

Let's get started on you becoming the best student and person you can be!

This year, you will learn steps you can take to succeed in your learning. You will look at the attributes that make an exemplary student.

- What does an exemplary teacher do?
- What are the four to six rules that will help my teacher and me succeed?
- What does positive energy look, sound, and feel like?
- What are my strengths?
- What are the skills needed to be successful in my learning?
- What is effort-based learning?
- How do I self-assess my learning?
- How does my brain work?
- What can I do to "train my brain and not let my brain train me"™ to do what is best for me?
- Why is asking questions on a concept so important to my success in learning?

And many more helpful ideas.

I believe all students can be successful in their learning. I will support you in this process. I know once you learn the tools you need and you train your brain™ to do what is best for you, anything is possible!

Please Score

On a scale of 0 to 8, please circle your score for this statement:

"I believe all students can be successful in their learning."

0 1 2 3 4 5 6 7 8

(0 is Not at all, and 8 is Absolutely.)

Discuss your scores with your class or someone else on why you recorded the score you did.

Effort equates to student success

SECTION I:
THE FIRST THREE WEEKS
OF SCHOOL

JOURNALS AND SELF-ASSESSMENTS

In the first few weeks of school, both you and your students will set up journals. You can document student effort in the various Education2Aspire attributes. You, (the student), should complete your first self-assessment. You'll discuss the ASPIRE attributes with your teacher or an adult, focusing on what each attribute can help you with in the classroom. Your teacher will keep a journal to be used for thoughts, ideas, and reflection. You will also keep a journal throughout the year to be used for recording your thoughts, ideas, goal setting, and concept understanding.

Your first self-assessment should ideally take place in the first week or two of the school year. Once the assessment is completed, your teacher can identify areas that may need to be worked on with you, and then goals can be set for different attributes. Lower elementary classrooms may want to set monthly goals in one of the areas, while weekly or biweekly goals may be set in upper elementary grades.

For example, you could put up a sign in the front of the classroom that reads "Achievement through Effort." (Posting ideas in the front of the room is particularly effective for visual learners but is helpful for all students.) Your teacher may state on Monday, "Students, this week we're going to work on training our brains to achieve through effort and hard work. We're going to work on finishing what we begin, sticking with a project until we complete it, learning from mistakes without considering them failures, staying focused on our goals, asking questions to make sure we understand our concepts, and not quitting even when our brain tells us to quit."

Students would then work for the whole week on this concept (teachers should be reminding their students multiple times per day that the class is working on effort.) A teacher may say something like, "Our concept today is *idioms*, but remember we're also working on effort and determination. We're going to stick with learning idioms until we

Fourth-Grade Student's Self-Reflection on the Attributes Learned from the Self-Assessment Sheet (See Appendices)

How did training your brain to emphasize and practice achievement through effort, a safe and respectful environment, and interdependence help you stay positive and become an exemplary student?

Student's response:
I think having effort has helped me because every day I go through a lot of stuff and having effort helps my life get easier and better. When I am going with my mom to go get the kids from school, I am able to stay calm and stay in the car until I get home. Having self-control has helped me because I sometimes get mad and I lose control. But when I can get calm and stay calm, I see myself not getting as mad.

15

understand what they are. Does anyone have a question about that?"

If a student is unsuccessful, both the student and teacher will be held accountable for reteaching and relearning the concept. This helps with reaffirming the belief that hard work and effort equate to a better learning outcome. At the end of the week, you should take about five minutes (in your reflective journals) to write a paragraph related to how you did in Achievement through Effort, including scoring yourself on a scale of zero to four.

Prior to the journal writing, you and your teacher, along with your class should have a conversation about the steps of journaling (record your thoughts; discuss in small groups or turn and talk to the person next to you; and then discuss as a complete class), as well as the scale and how you should assess yourself on achievement through effort.

> 4—indicates a student *always* used the attributes needed for effort
> 3—means the student used the attributes needed for effort *most of the time*
> 2—indicates the student used the attributes needed for effort *some of the time*
> 1—indicates the student *rarely* used the attributes needed for effort
> 0—means the student felt he or she *never* used the attributes for effort

A score of zero should come up only very rarely in your classroom. With encouragement and hard work, you should be at a two or greater in your scoring. The best approach is to speak your effort scores out loud to help align both your interpretation and your teacher's interpretation of your efforts. Sharing scores out loud emphasizes accountability for expectations and helps your you achieve an awareness of the expectations you have for yourself. Your teacher should record the scores you (and the class) call out so they have a good understanding of who is committing their best efforts and who may need more support.

It may also be helpful to have feedback given about your effort score, especially at the beginning of the school year. For example, a student might say, "I was a four today in effort." A teacher might say, "I disagree. You were talking to another student, who then couldn't focus. When you take focus from other students, they may lose the opportunity to learn the concept we're working on. So I see your score as a three." "Do you agree with me?" The goal is to clarify how a four is earned when the student supports the learning of others by not distracting another student. Your teacher should let you know they aren't trying to discount what you believe your score should be. If you still want a four, your teacher may give it to you because the self-assessment process is about growth. However, your teacher should add, "Do you understand what is expected tomorrow to receive a score of four?"

Once a baseline self-assessment is established early in the year, discuss your goals for each attribute and then conduct further assessments at the middle and end of the year. For these assessments, it's important to discuss the scores from each one, especially if they are different from your teacher's score for you. In lower grades, the assessments could be conducted with a short conversation, because you may be just starting to understand the meaning of each attribute of learning success.

Use your reflective journals to document your conceptual understanding, effort, goal setting, and self-actualization. Set goals at the beginning of the year for each subject area or the specific subject being taught that period. Ask your teacher if they could provide scores from last year's state tests. For example, in Minneapolis Public Schools, teachers gave the Northwest Evaluation Association's Measures of Academic Progress (MAP) tests for math and reading at the beginning, middle, and end of the academic year. Administering the tests in that sequence allowed students and teachers to see their measurable growth in these subjects. The students' improvement demonstrates how valuable the ASPIRE attributes can be to their academic success.

Discuss your goals in your journal and how you can achieve each one, using a template such as, "here is where I am; here is where I want to be; here is how I will get there." You will be creating a concrete structure for your success that can reinforce the idea that you can train your brain to be successful. Training your brain is crucial

You will do this self-assessment three times to see how you improve on these attributes over the school year.

I believe if you work hard to gain these attributes, you will learn all that is possible in this school year.

17

Training their brains is crucial because it helps students understand that the brain can be trained to consistently focus on positive, effort-driven thoughts rather than the self-defeating inner dialogue of giving up or failure.

You can also use your journal for proof of concept. In math, for example, a student can use pictures, explanations, or problem statements to reflect on a new topic. Your teacher may ask you to explain a new idea by posing a journal question—for example, "What is area?" Whenever your teacher describes or discusses a concept, you can write down how you understand that concept in your journals. Underline key components of your understanding, then turn and talk to another student to see how their thinking compares to their neighbors'. Then discuss that concept as a class.

Overall, using the journals in this interactive way encourages you to learn from each other through a high degree of classroom interaction, which will help keep you focused on a specific concept. It also concretely demonstrates the value of cooperation and working together because the entire class will be comparing notes. The process also accommodates a need to look at specific students' understanding of a concept to determine if they need additional academic support. Also, since the journals are essentially a way to read your thoughts after each lesson, this practice allows your teacher to refine their teaching methods by gathering information about which methods are working and which are less effective in creating understanding for you.

You might also pick a single ASPIRE attribute to focus on in a given week's or month's journals. (Teachers, if you're teaching third grade or younger, you might select one or two attributes to focus on. In grades four and five, add in a few more, and in grade six and higher, the class can focus, in turn, on each and every Education2Aspire attribute).

The guiding idea for the journals is that you routinely train yourself to think about the specific processes you will use to achieve a goal as you improve toward it. Even with students as young as kindergarten or first grade, you can train your brain to learn ten new words each week. One scaffolding strategy for this goal is to learn words that share the same suffix or sound similar to one another. Your teacher may ask if you can think of any ideas to help achieve the goal of learning ten new words per week.

Consider applying the same collective approach to behavior. In a classroom that has a hard time staying on task, you could challenge your yourself to work and focus for five uninterrupted minutes. Try again if or when you fail the first few times. Failure is a lesson, if you learn from it. Use the Adult Think Out Loud approach to demonstrate. For example, your teacher may say, "Class, as we've discussed, our goal is to focus for five minutes. What can we do this time that we didn't do in our first try?" The students may say things like, "We can remind each other to stay focused," and "One of us can stand by you and go to another student if they're not focused," and so on. The point here is for you to start understanding that you're able to solve problems on your own, with a teacher's guidance when needed. Your teacher is always trying to empower their students to solve their own problems. This will help students know they have the capability for solving their own problems or know when more help may be needed.

Exemplary teachers want strong-thinking, empowered, and confident students; they're trying to develop students who think, "I know I can solve this problem." Regardless of the goal, make sure to celebrate when you achieve it. Also have a conversation with your teacher if you don't achieve the goal. The aim isn't just achieving a specific goal (e.g., five uninterrupted minutes of collective focus), but modeling effective goal setting and learning that ongoing effort is a key to success. You should understand that failure is part of obtaining a goal. Not reaching a goal is not necessarily failure, because it can serve as a lesson and an opportunity to try again.

Beyond the weekly progress reports and in-class discussions with students about their self-assessments, I encourage you to use the Education2Aspire assessment and scoring system to track progress showing effort. Record the assessments of effort by period or by subject matter each day. This type of continuous tracking allows your teacher to identify if you may need more intervention in your learning effort. It's an important way for you and your teacher to monitor your effort and its results over time.

Use your journal to record how much effort you are putting into your learning each day. I believe if you give your best effort, you will have a great learning year. In each subject of the day, train your brain™ to do your best effort.

Score yourself using the self-assessments on page 24 and 25 to show how you are doing in each subject each day of this school year.

Example: Math 5, Social Studies 7, Gym 2, Music 5, Language Arts 6, Science 6, and so on . . .

HOW TO SELF-ACTUALIZE AND RECORD THOUGHTS:

The first thing to learn about in gaining success is to **set goals** to achieve an end result you would like to happen.

The steps for setting goals are:

- Where am I now?
- Where would I like to be?
- How do I get there?

If you complete these steps for each of your subjects throughout the school year, you will have more success in each of these subjects.

Most successful entrepreneurs look at what is needed in their surroundings. Can the entrepreneur come up with a new or better idea within their community? Can they make an exciting product better? Once the entrepreneur identifies the idea, they think, What steps do I need to do to get this idea implemented?

Businesses also set goals to succeed. Businesses will hire industrial engineers to assist in setting goals like *"What is needed that is not being done now?" "What can be improved on, and how can it be improved?"*

Write your goals each of your subjects in a notebook or journal.

Example Goal: Math

Where am I now -
I am a B student.

Where would I like to be? -
I would like to be an A student.

How do I get there?

1. *I will meet with students in my class that are A students after school to discuss the concepts.*

2. *I will go online to look at work in the concept we are studying.*

3. *I will go to my teacher for additional information when I do not fully understand a concept.*

4. *I will ask questions when in my math class. I am proving I understand the concept being taught that day.*

5. *I know it is my responsibility to ask as many questions as needed to get to an understanding of the concept.*

6. *I will ask the teacher to explain the concept in a different way if I do not under stand the concept.*

SET A GOAL FOR YOUR SUBJECT:

1. This is where I am

2. This is where I would like to be

3. This is how I will get to my goal

Write down your thoughts about the above questions in the space below or in your journal. Then discuss your list with the students around you, and add any new ideas to your list.

DIFFERENT LEARNING STYLES:

We have **three different learning styles**, and most of us learn best in one of these three styles of learning.

VISUAL LEARNER:

You learn best by seeing things.

AUDITORY LEARNER:

You learn best by hearing things.

KINESTHETIC LEARNER:

You learn best by feeling or experiencing things.

Which type of learning style do you think works best for you?

If your teacher is teaching in one learning style, what can you do to have them also teach in your learning style?

With your teacher, discuss as a class, and add any additional ideas to your list.

Knowing your learning style is very important for you. If you are having trouble learning an idea or concept, it may be because you are not using the correct learning style for you!

It is very important to ask your teacher if they can teach an idea or concept in your learning style if you are having a difficult time.

Remember, your job is to ask questions until you understand the idea or concept. Never give up!

Examples:

Visual:
Some students can learn them by seeing a picture of $2 \times 6 = 12$, which are two rows of six objects.

$$000000$$
$$000000 = 12$$

Auditory:
In school, you learn your multiplication tables. Some students can memorize them by saying them over and over until they know $2 \times 6 = 12$.

Kinesthetic:
Some students would like to have connecting blocks or squares to touch to learn $2 \times 6 = 12$.

Write down an example of a subject or concept you recently learned about in class.

What learning style did your teacher teach it in?

If it was not taught in your learning style, how could it have been taught in the style that best helps you?

Remember to use these steps when learning a concept. Write your thoughts in a notebook or journal.

1. Think about the concept by yourself.
2. Discuss the concept with a group or partner.
3. Discuss the concept with your class and teacher.

Remember to keep asking questions until you understand the concept! Your job is to ask the questions until you have an understanding, and your teacher's job is to keep trying different learning styles until you have understanding!

Remember: Effort will give you success in your learning!

Student's Daily Self-Assessment

Student Name:_____ Advisory: _____

Grade: _____   Date from: _____ to: _____

Train your brain, don't let your brain train you™

Scoring:	7 - 8	5 - 6	3 - 4	1 - 2	0
	Always	Most of the Time	Sometimes	Rarely	Never

Attribute I am working on: _____

X = *In my seat on time with materials needed for my class out and ready.*

Class Period	Monday		Tuesday		Wednesday		Thursday		Friday	
Hour 1										
Hour 2										
Hour 3										
Hour 4										
Hour 5										
Hour 6										
Hour 7										
Advisory										

Self-Reflection

What I did to train my brain this week: _____

_____

_____

Parent Signature: _____

You have permission to copy as needed.

Student's Daily Self-Assessment

Student Name:_____ Advisory: _____

Grade: _____   Date from: _____ to: _____

Train your brain, don't let your brain train you™

Scoring:	7 - 8	5 - 6	3 - 4	1 - 2	0
	Always	Most of the Time	Sometimes	Rarely	Never

Attribute I am working on: _____

| X | = *In my seat on time with materials needed for my class out and ready.*

Class Period	Monday		Tuesday		Wednesday		Thursday		Friday	
Hour 1										
Hour 2										
Hour 3										
Hour 4										
Hour 5										
Hour 6										
Hour 7										
Advisory										

Self-Reflection

What I did to train my brain this week: _____

_____

_____

Parent Signature: _____

You have permission to copy as needed.

Dear Mr. Jone

Your agreat teacher.
When I was in 4th grade I wanted
to be in your class and I did.
I hope you and JO can be
together forever until you dead.
5th grade is amazing because you
are my teacher and you made a
better and person and smarter.
Thank you Mr. Jone!

From Dominique your Best
student.

Here are some cards from my students on their experience and their learning process in my classroom.

Dear Mr. Jones,
  Mr. Jones I'll always remember you. My favorite thing you did was give us PUNishments. You were always great because you're never mad at us, you say our brains tricks us. I will remember you most for your great enthusiasm. I'll never forget you.

                              Sincerely,
                              Giovanni
                              Green

Dear Mr. Jones,

I think your a fun teacher and I like when you say your brain is tricking you I also like when you gave us the super hero story

Project
                    Your student,
                    Jazmine

Dear, Mr. Jones
        It was fun when you were our science teacher.
I liked the jokes and Jim and Jon story. I liked the
experiments we did and I will miss you when you retire.
I wish you a happy life after being a teacher.
                         Sincerely,
                         Buweyda

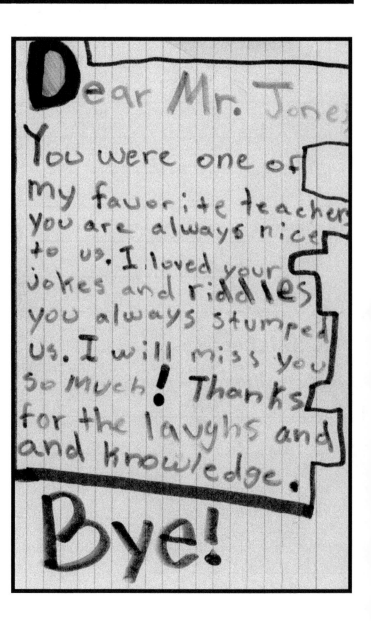

An Exemplary Student

Make a list of all the things an exemplary student does. Use the space on this page.

(If doing this as a class, make and post a poster of an exemplary student)

Your thoughts:

28

Now discuss your list with the students around you, and add any new ideas to your list.

Next, with your teacher, discuss as a class, and add any additional ideas to your list.

MY THOUGHTS ON WHAT AN EXEMPLARY STUDENT SHOULD DO:

1. Asks questions to help them learn concepts and ideas.

2. Never gives up their effort.

3. Knows they can find a solution to a problem if they don't stop working on the problem.

4. Stays focused on the work at hand.

5. Learns from their mistakes, and the mistakes become lessons that they learn from.

6. Always gives their best effort in their work.

7. Respects themselves and others.

8. Works to find solutions to conflicts.

9. Is eager to explore new things and ideas.

10. Is prepared for their learning.

11. Is on time for class.

12. Completes their homework on time.

13. Does their best work.

14. Says what they think in a respectful way.

15. Is a good listener so that they learn from others.

16. Works cooperatively with others to be successful in their learning.

17. Is willing to pass their knowledge on to others.

18. Has enthusiasm for their learning.

19. Can focus and not be distracted by others.

20. Remains calm, doing what is right for themselves and others.

21. Has an appreciation for the opportunities that come to them.

22. Has empathy for others.

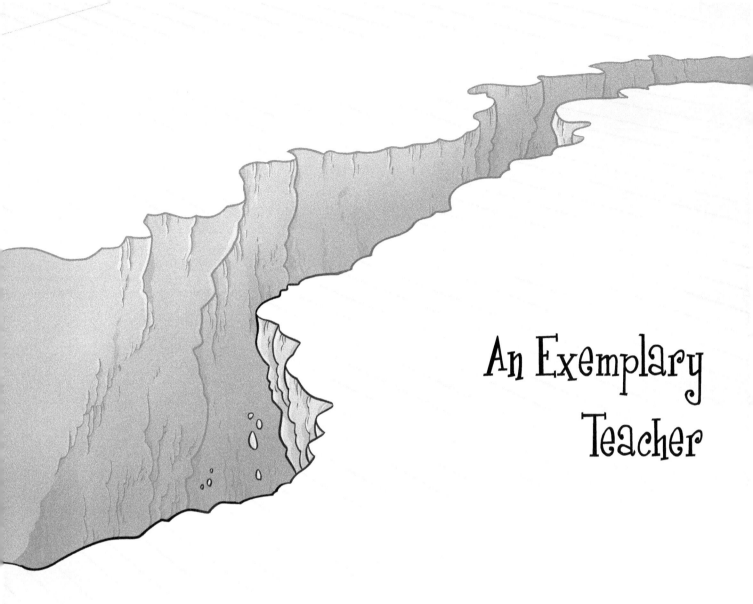

An Exemplary Teacher

Make a list of all the things an exemplary teacher does. Use the space on this page.

(If doing this as a class, make and post a poster of an exemplary teacher)

Your thoughts:

Now discuss your list with the students around you, and add any new ideas to your list.

Next, with your teacher, discuss as a class, and add any additional ideas to your list.

AN EXEMPLARY TEACHER DOES THE FOLLOWING:

1. Has a belief that all students can learn.

2. Is excited about the subjects they are teaching to their students.

3. Works to know each student's strengths and weaknesses.

4. Is prepared to teach their classes each day.

5. Is on time for class.

6. Has all the materials they need to do their work.

7. Takes a personal interest in each student's life and the student's learning.

8. Teaches the students in all the different learning styles.

9. Makes sure all students understand the concepts that are being taught.

10. Explains what they are doing and why they are doing it, so the students can learn and understand from the teacher's thinking.

11. Challenges every student to think deeply in the concepts the student is learning.

12. Supports and scaffolds the students learning so that they do not quit on their learning.

13. Takes the time to do something fun each day. Example: I liked to do Wuzzles, or riddles, with my students at the beginning of class. It was fun and joyful for me, and the students enjoyed the challenge of figuring out the Wuzzles.

14. Ends each class with a summary of what was learned in the class.

15. Conducts a random survey of three or four students to see if the students understand the concepts they worked on learning that day.

16. Doesn't get mad at the student. They are mad at the choice or decision of the student.

17. Always brings their best selves to the class.

18. Sees and treats the behavior of students the same as any other subject to be learned.

Now you will make the bridge between what an exemplary student does and the rules needed to help them succeed in their learning. Write four to six rules in the space below.

YOUR THOUGHTS ABOUT RULES:

Now discuss your list with the students around you, and add any new ideas to your list.

Next, with your teacher, discuss as a class, and add any additional ideas to your list.

I use the word bridge because the rules that you, your teacher, and the class create will be a bridge between the rules and what the exemplary student needs to help them learn.

Here are my thouughts about the rules:

1. Be respectful to yourself, others, and materials.

2. Do your best work all the time.

3. Raise your hand to talk, and listen to others as they talk.

4. Ask questions of the teacher or other students so that you always understand the concepts being taught.

5. Be prepared for class with homework and materials needed, and be in your seat at the start of class.

Are your thoughts similar?

The room you're in just is! We will make the energy in this room by our actions. To do this, we need to know what positive energy coming from people **looks, sounds, and feels like**. Use the space on this page to record your thoughts.

YOUR THOUGHTS ABOUT POSITIVE ENERGY:

Now discuss your list with the students around you, and add any new ideas to your list.

Next, with your teacher, discuss as a class, and add any additional ideas to your list.

Positive energy **LOOKS** like:

People are cooperating with a common goal, they are focused on the task at hand, respect is given and received by everyone. You see people listening to one another, and everyone is valued in their thoughts and ideas. People know their strengths and weaknesses in learning. We help one another succeed in their learning. People are smiling at one another, and they may even sing with joy.

Positive energy **SOUNDS** like:

laughter, excitement, each person uses their accountable talk, they are sharing ideas, everyone has a chance to talk about what they think.

Positive energy **FEELS** like:

love, strength, joy, respect, happiness, and an I-can-do-it attitude.

I had signs in my room to remind my students about our belief in one another. The sign says the following things:

> # *We all have a gift to share!*
>
> *Celebrate one another's gifts!*
> *Find your talent! Share your gift with others!*
> *What will your gift be to others?*

Cooperative Group Work

$\mathcal{C}$ooperative group exercises are an important way to build cooperation and collaboration in the classroom. They're designed to get students to listen to each other and to discuss strategies for completing a task. Students will learn to value their own thinking and the thinking of their peers. I propose groups of four for each cooperative group, divided among these roles:

- **Leader**—makes sure each student has a specific task to do. They are also responsible for making sure each member of the group is heard.

- **Recorder**—writes down ideas and solutions to the problem.

- **Reporter**—presents the group's findings to the classroom and organizes how to present those findings.

- **Positive person**—uses positive statements to acknowledge others in the group and notices positive statements made by other group members.

I once had a student named Gavin who was a highly talented and successful student in and out of school. I felt it was my responsibility to challenge his thinking at a much deeper level and help him think outside the box so he had the ability to create new and different ideas. In one of our self-actualization meetings, Gavin told me, "I know the other students look at me as a leader, but I'd like to learn how to step back and be a better listener to other students, giving them a chance to be the leader of our cooperative groups." This showed me the deep reflection Gavin had on who he was and who he wanted to be. It also provided encouraging evidence that my students were reflecting and expanding their thinking.'

After you complete the assigned task, each group in your classroom will get up and present its findings to the whole class." Some of the skills you and other students should focus on are:

- Groups should use accountable talk, allowing each person to share their information. Or the presenter shares, and then others have an opportunity to add on with their thoughts.

- Make sure to speak in loud clear voice, so everyone can hear you.

- If the person writing the information on the poster or paper wants to create graphics that help explain your concept, do so after each group presentation.

- You and other students can then make comments about what they did well or give constructive criticism of what they could do better.

- The positive person should explain to the group what everyone did and if anyone was hurt.

- Remember when a group is reporting, clapping and acknowledging the group effort is important. All your comments are done in the spirit of cooperation and support to improve student success. Remember, we're all working together to improve our learning skills.

- Ensure that none of the statements—from the teacher, the class, or the positive person—are done with a spirit of meanness or negativity. Stress to students that everyone is in this together, another Education2Aspire cornerstone.

Cooperative projects are a great way to foster your appreciation and approaches to sharing your ideas. I would suggest you do one to two of these cooperate projects each month

---

What do you think the meaning of the following statement is?

"Two heads are better than one!"

Record your thoughts below.

Working in cooperative groups will help you have the skills needed in a job and your learning. About 70 percent of people that are promoted are promoted because they work well with others. The reverse is also true; about 70 percent of people fired from a job do not work well with others. When you work together, you have more ideas, and the tasks are completed faster and better.

You deserve to learn the skills of how to work together. To help you gain that skill, I will first explain the main roles in cooperative groups. They are recorder, reporter, positive person, and leader. At first, it is okay to pick the role you like to do, but eventually, doing all the positions is important. Remember, you will always feel most comfortable in your strengths! You will want to work on all areas so that when you have a job, you will feel you can do any role the boss asks of you.

The classroom is a safe place to learn these cooperative skills. The recorder writes down what the group agrees is the answer. All the members of the group's input and ideas are valued. The reporter shares the results with the room. The positive person encourages the group. The leader makes sure all members of the group state their thoughts. The leader also will ask each team member if they have anything to add. In this way, all team members feel valued.

I believe it is a good idea to do some type of project that shows you are part of the class and have ownership in how the room works. This project can be anything that shows your name in the room. My classes did a Name Art Project, but there are many different projects that can be done.

Activities and Strategies to Foster a Positive Classroom

The M&M Activity

You or your teacher will pick a person to do this activity with. You will arm-wrestle with your partner. In this activity, each time you get the student's hand to touch the table, you get one M&M. Then go back to the starting position and try to get a second M&M and so on for 20 seconds. How many M&M's can you get before time runs out?

Every person receives some M&M's for their effort.

HAVE FUN AND BE SAFE.
DO NOT HURT ANYONE BY PUSHING TOO HARD!

READY, SET, GO!

- Did more than one person per team receive a great deal of M&M's?

- What was the goal of this activity? Was the goal to see who the strongest person was or to get as many M&M's as possible?

- What is best way to get as many M&M's as possible?

Discuss your results with the students around you, and record any new ideas. Then, with your teacher discuss as a class and write down any additional ideas

The goal was to receive as many M&M's as possible. To do this, you would need to work together. You would let your partner put your hand down, and then they would let you put their hand down. This would allow you both to receive many M&M's.

There are many thoughts I have about this activity! It is very important to read questions on tests and in discussion so that you answer the question that is being asked of you.

How many of you were trying to win by being the strongest?

Working together allows us to accomplish so much more! This will be true for us this year in your learning. The more we work together, helping one another succeed, the better results we will all get in our learning.And the opposite is true also, the more we push against each other the less we accomplish in our learning.

If you remember your job is to ask as many questions as you need to understand a problem in math or information in any class. The teacher's job is to explain the problem in as many learning styles as needed.

If you and your teacher work together you can learn anything well!

46

The Hula Hoop Activity

Your teacher will put you in groups of four to six students.

First, place the Hula-Hoop on the arm of one of the students. Each of you are to grasp hands and not let go. When your team has it back to the first person, everyone will bend down. The first team to bend down without letting go of one another's hands wins that round.

Now each team discusses how to improve their movement of the Hula-Hoop around the circle (the time given for discussion should be about one to two minutes). After the time is up, teams should try again.

HAVE FUN AND BE SAFE.
DO NOT HURT ANYONE BY PUSHING TOO HARD!

READY, SET, GO!

Do you have a different winner?
Repeat about four to six times.

Which team won?

YOUR THOUGHTS:

Write your thoughts on why the team won:

Write your thoughts on what your team could have done better.

The Paper Tower Build

Materials needed:

- one yard of masking tape
- three full sheets of newspaper

You will be in teams of two, three, or four students.

All teams have _____ time to build as tall of a tower as possible, using the masking tape and sheets of newspaper provided. The tower must stand on its own for at least one minute.

HAVE FUN AND BE SAFE.
DO NOT HURT ANYONE BY PUSHING TOO HARD!

READY, SET, GO!

Discuss as a group what made a good tower and record your answers below or in your journal.

What did you learn from your team?

What did you learn about yourself in this activity?

Is there anything you can do to improve your tower?

The Paper Tower Build is a great activity to see if you and your peers can work together. This activity helps us see the attributes we all use to succeed in life and in our learning.

Positive attributes:

- not giving up

- listening to one another

- finding what way works best and then emulating that way

- trusting one another to do their best

- helping one another to get better

- asking for help from the person that is doing it the fastest or best way.

Negative attributes:

- quitting on yourself and your team

- yelling at others

- not looking to others for the answer on how to do the activity better and faster

- not trying to do your best

Cooperation is a very important part of any team's success. We see examples of this everywhere in our lives; the football team where the linemen block, the quarterback hands the ball off well, and the running back makes a touchdown or the basketball player makes a great screen for her teammate and the teammate scores. The band members each practice their instruments for hours and then have a great concert.

I would tell each of you to try to **be the best team player you can be!** This is not only so your class and teacher can succeed but you as well!

Chess is like life!

I liked to have every student play chess each week for about forty-five minutes. I would have a chess master come in to teach the class the basic moves and a few strategies of the game. Chess teaches students to think more deeply, to consider how an immediate choice will affect them later. Each move they make on the board will influence their future moves. I observed that our weekly chess matches helped my students make fewer impulsive decisions. It taught them the value of careful longer-term thinking.

Dear Mr. Jones,
I really don't want you to retire !!
I'm really sorry you couldn't be at
Pillsbury for the 5th graders next
year. But on the bright spot you've
made lots of kids happy over the
years !! Good luck with your career
after you retire !!

Thanks For Everything—
Natalie

Inspiration for Extra-credit Activities

Superhero Stories

I would like to invite you to make a comic book in which you are the superhero. Several times I had a cartoonist come into the school and draw each of the students as the superhero they created in their stories. The cartoonist's drawing was then placed on the cover of the student's story. My students found this project particularly exciting. They would all choose to do it, and they were thrilled to have such a great keepsake. I've also done this project in conjunction with a media specialist who found an online interface that allowed the students to transform their stories into a comic-book format.

Make Your Own Country

You will design and describe a country of your own invention. Determine the type of government, the laws, what products the country manufactures, where the country is located, who its dignitaries are, its history, and so on. You can either draw your country or make a model of it. One of my students made an underwater country. A city was placed on a plywood board and the entire city was covered with Plexiglas to illustrate that it was on the ocean floor.

Design a Paper Airplane

I would like to invite you to make paper airplanes and pitting them against one another in simple, friendly challenges: Which one can do the largest loop-de-loop? Which airplane can fly the farthest? Which one can land the most accurately? Which plane has the most interesting design? You can make a different airplane for each challenge. After the the different challenges are complete, have a discussion about why each airplane looks or functions the way it does.

Science Experiments

I created a packet with many ideas for science experiments, and I also encouraged students to find interesting experiments themselves on the Internet. Pick one to share. In their papers, you should describe how to conduct the experiment and discuss why you choose the experiment.

Teacher of the Day

I would like to invite you to make something you know well and love doing to teach your peers. Write a several-page informational sheet on your topic. For example, my students taught things like how to dribble a basketball, what equipment is required to ride a horse, and how to make brownies. This assignment allows you to show your individual strengths to your peers. This was one strategy in my ongoing efforts to help students see themselves as important to the class and to the larger community. I'm convinced that each student who completed this project left our classroom with greater self-esteem, which I believe helps students build happier and healthier life experiences.

Rube Goldberg Machines

I would like to invite you to make your own Rube Goldberg machine—a device that intentionally uses a complex series of actions to perform a simple task, usually incorporating a chain reaction. You can build or draw your inventions, or do both. You should also create a one-page explanation about what the Goldberg machine does and describe why you chose to design in just this way.

Making Robots

I would like to invite you to draw a robot or make one out of boxes, computer parts, and the like. Write about what the robot does and why you choose that task. For example, one of my students brought in a robot made with his father's help. The robot had a body made of a metal garbage can—the head was a bucket, the eyes and mouth had lighting with cord to plug into the outlet, and the arms and legs were metal duct material.

The Word List

I would like to invite you to find ten new words you like or think are interesting. Then write out the words and their definitions and then create sentences that used the words. Make a large word wall where you can place a few of your favorite words. Each successive week, pick a few words to concentrate on using during that week. By the end of the year, you should have used all the words.

Soap Art

I would like to invite you to design on paper, a sculpture you want to make out of soap. You sould write about what the design is and why you want to make that design. (Using soap is safer than carving wood, which requires a sharp knife.)

Other Project Ideas

Make your own magazine; write a joke and share it with your peers; perform an end-of-the-year play; Fermi problems; draw a picture and write a story to go with it; and draw pictures of buildings in your area and write information about these buildings.

Activities and Strategies to Foster a Positive Classroom

Gratitude List

I would like to invite you to take time each morning to list three things that you are grateful for to develop an appreciation for what you have and are given.

Emotional-Wellness Activities

These projects can help you feel some ownership of the room, which can help you understand that you have rights and obligations within your school, classroom, and the world around you. For example, at the very end of a period, your teacher can conduct a two- to five-minute emotional-wellness activity. The activity could be a short game, a puzzle, fun reading (e.g., a Shel Silverstein excerpt), poems, or something as simple as social time. Even though a few minutes of daily learning time is "lost" by doing this, it will help you understand that if you work hard for forty minutes during work time, you'll be rewarded with a fun activity or social time at the end. Students are less likely to chat with one another during a lesson if they know they will have this time later. The short socialization time can also free up the teacher to meet with students who may have a concern about a concept in the subject or who need to have a discussion about behavioral expectations. This short time at the end of a period allows for a clean and clear start for next class period.

Passing Notes

One example of a fun social activity is note passing at the end of a period. Students love to do this anyway, so it's naturally fun for them. I tell students to write to other students in the classroom saying something positive and to sign the note. I discuss that no note can be passed that isn't signed. I also instruct them to not talk as they move around the room. If the students don't follow this instruction, they must either sit by me or I stop the activity. We then discuss how to be successful next time with the activity. (This is useful because students are modeling reflecting on something that didn't work and how to make it work. They may say things like, "If a student is talking, send them to another room so they miss the activity.") While the notes were being passed, I would write notes of support to students I think will benefit from them. I write things such as, "Great job of asking questions today in your learning. I can see you're using the strategies we've been working on to learn. Keep up the great work!" These words of encouragement mean a great deal to the students.

Who's Missing?

Strengthening the connection between students is also important for the emotional wellness of a classroom. Playing the game "Who's Missing?" is one way to do that. Have two students leave the room (and perhaps have a third student watch to make sure they don't look into the classroom and spoil the game). While the two students are out of the room, have the rest of the class move to different desks and ask one student to hide in a closet or behind the teacher's desk. Once everyone is in position, have the two students come back into the room. Ask them to figure out who's hiding in one minute or with five guesses, whichever comes first. Even if they don't guess correctly or they run out of time, have the hidden student enthusiastically pop out from a hiding spot. The game will strengthen bonds between classmates.

The Eraser Game

This game teaches students to develop a sense of fun and "team" in a classroom. Divide the class into two teams and have a representative from each team stand on either side of the classroom with an eraser balanced on his or her head. When the teacher says, "Go," one student tries to tag the other while both try to keep their erasers on their heads. If someone's eraser falls off or he or she gets tagged, the opposing team gets a point, and whichever team has the most points after five minutes wins the game. Every fifteen to twenty seconds, the teacher can say, "Reverse," and the chasing student becomes the chaser.

Can I Trick You?

This game encourages you to think outside the box. Before escorting students to the lunchroom, tell them that if nobody in the room talks on the way there, you will receive five dollars. As the class walks down the hall, the teacher should make a point of talking to the class or to you as you walk and saying hello to as many teachers and administrators as possible, and excitedly ask the students to say hello too. Assuming you make it all the way to the lunchroom without talking, as it turns out, someone WAS talking talking the whole time—the teacher! (Make sure to have a treat prepared so there are no hard feelings.)

The idea behind this game—other than playing a lighthearted prank on you—is to encourage you to think outside the box and examine your teacher's statements and instructions carefully. Another example involves holding up a hand and asking a someone in the the room, "How many fingers do I have?" They may say five or four, depending on if they're counting your thumb. You could respond with, "No, I have eight fingers and two thumbs!" These kinds of question help you to listen more carefully and help you to think deeper about questions in general.

Teacher's Journal

The end goal of these strategies is to create an environment where the teacher and students are working together under the belief that they both want what is best for each other. The emotions and feelings that are cultivating in a classroom should be laughter, joy, focus, stimulation, excitement, and a can-do spirit. This is why the "exemplary student" and "exemplary teacher" posters discussed early on can be so helpful in an Education2Aspire classroom: the student knows what an exemplary student does and tries to emulate that behavior. The teacher is then able to support students' learning by assessing their efforts and ensuring they're progressing closer and closer to the ideal posted on the classroom wall. If teachers help students gain the skills of an exemplary student, they can then put those skills to use in their learning.

It is valuable to keep a classroom list that teachers can use to write short notes as they observe students. I used that information to help me assess what each student needed academically and behaviorally. I also advocate that teachers spend five to ten minutes each evening writing short reflections to help them decide which practices to use the next day. My journal documented activities and strategies that worked in the classroom, emotional activities that were needed, emotional conflicts that may have occurred between teachers or students, the positive things that were going on within the classroom, or issues that needed to be looked at or addressed that were blocking some students' learning. Here is a quick-and-dirty way to gauge this: if I felt energized and positive at the end of the day, I could be fairly confident that it was a successful day for my students and me; if I was emotionally drained, it usually meant I needed to reconsider the strategies I was using.

The Daily Forecast

To foster an emotionally supportive classroom, talk about any rituals or routines that are new or changing. Regardless of which rules are established, make sure to be positive and energetic throughout these activities—smiling helps a lot too. Students should excitedly wonder which fun way the class will start or end each day. In addition, no matter how difficult the class is for you, a short, fun activity at the start and end of the period will help you feel an emotional connection to the classroom, which can make you excited to come back and prepared to try to learn, even if the class material is difficult.

Good-News Board

Another engaging activity to incorporate into an Education2Aspire classroom is a good-news board. The board should have a space near the classroom door or entryway where anyone can write down enjoyable, interesting, or otherwise positive news from the past twenty-four hours. You can initial your individual pieces of good news before you enter the classroom, which can help you focus on something positive and feel a sense of ownership. For example, "Last night,

I went to a concert, and I had a great time!" As often as possible, stand at the door as students enter and have quick conversations about the good news they post. (Have several markers or other writing utensils available so more than one student at a time can share good news.)

I had a student who was quiet and shy and did not speak much. One day, she wrote about some music she enjoyed on our class good-news board. I asked her to say more about this music, because she clearly had a vested interest in it. She told the rest of the class and me about music and why she liked it. Each day after that, she would share more and more music information with the class, and she gradually felt more empowered and important. The good-news board gave her an avenue to talk about something important to her and allowed her to have a deeper connection with her classmates and me.

Keep It Moving

Movement-centered activities also help students focus emotionally and academically. If a teacher encourages a kinetic activity at least once per day, students know they'll have a chance to get up and move, which will help them be more focused on their work during the lesson in the meantime. Games like Simon Says allow this type of strategic movement opportunity.

MULTIPLE INTELLIGENCES

We all have skills to share in the world! Each of us can make a difference by sharing our skills with others.

The following are Howard Gardner's Multiple Intelligences. Howard Gardner is an American developmental psychologist at Harvard University.

On page 59, write down what you believe are your skills. Look at each of the skills on page 58 and circle those you believe you have to share with others. Please discuss your skills with your groups, classroom, or some other person.

LOGIC SMART
Math-Logical Intelligence

Think: by reasoning/problem-solving

Love: math, experimenting, questioning, figuring out logic puzzles, calculation, etc.

Need: things to explore and think about, science materials, manipulatives, experiments, trips (science museums, planetarium), etc.

SELF-SMART
Intrapersonal Intelligence

Think: deeply inside of themselves

Love: setting goals, mediating, dreaming, being quiet, planning, etc.

Need: time alone, self-paced projects, choices, time to reflect and think, etc.

WORD SMART
Linguistic Intelligence

Think: in oral and written words

Love: talking, reading, writing, telling stories, spelling, playing word games, etc.

Need: books, tapes, writing tools, diaries, discussion, stories, etc.

PICTURE SMART
Spatial Intelligence

Think: in images and pictures

Love: designing, drawing, visualizing, doodling, etc.

Need: art, videos, movies, slides, imagination games, mazes, puzzles, illustrated books, LEGOs, trips to art museums, etc.

PEOPLE SMART
Interpersonal Intelligence

Think: by bouncing ideas off other people

Love: leading, organizing, relating, manipulating, mediating, etc.

Need: friends, group games, social gatherings, community events, clubs, mentors/apprenticeships, etc.

MUSIC SMART
Musical Intelligence

Think: through rhymes and melodies

Love: singing, whistling, humming, tapping feet, clapping hands, listening, playing instruments, etc.

Need: sing-along time, trips to concerts, music playing at home and school, musical instruments, etc.

BODY SMART
Bodily Kinesthetic Intelligence

- **Think**: through things that affect one's body

- **Love**: running, jumping, building, touching, gesturing, dancing, etc.

- **Need**: role-play, drama, movement, things to build, sports, and physical games, tactile experiences, hands-on learning, etc.

NATURALIST SMART
Nature Intelligence

Think: are often keenly aware of their surroundings and changes in their environments, even if these shifts are at minute or subtle levels.

Love: looking at human behaviors or the behaviors and habitats of other species.

Need: must be outside playing, looking, seeking, getting their hands dirty, and spending time exploring nature.

Write down the skills you think best represent you:

Discuss your skills with the students around you, and add any new ideas to your list.

Next, with your teacher, discuss as a class what each student's skills are, and add any additional ideas to your list.

Can you learn to do anything?

YOUR THOUGHTS:

Discuss your list with the students around you, and add any new ideas to your list.

Next, with your teacher, discuss as a class, and add any additional ideas to your list.

Believe you can learn anything! Here's an example - When we are babies, we need to learn to walk. We start by crawling, then we get up on our legs and try to walk, and we fall down. We get back up and so on until that amazing day when we are walking. That is a learned behavior! We never gave up on learning how to walk. We are all A+ walkers unless we have a physical disability.

Believe if you try to learn and keep getting up when you fall, you can learn anything!

YOUR THOUGHTS:

Can you give an example of something you did that other people said you couldn't do and you still did it?

Did you have to keep trying to get it done?

Are you better at it the more you do it?

Who is smart?

Write down your thoughts about the questions below on the following page. Use your journal if you need more space to write.

Justify your answer with "Yes, because" or "No, because."

1. Is the first one done the smartest?

2. Are you smart if you ask questions?

3. Can you learn to do things well?

4. Does prior knowledge help in your understanding of concepts and the world around you?

5. Is the first student done on a test the smartest?

6. Does trying something and failing help you in your understanding of the world?

YOUR THOUGHTS:

1.

2.

3.

4.

5.

6.

Your brain learns best when you are asking questions. It makes your brain create the pathways to understanding concepts. ***It is your responsibility to ask questions to help in your learning***. You may be thinking, What? I don't understand! Ask your teacher to repeat what they are saying or to teach it in a different learning style. ***It is your teacher's responsibility to teach to your learning style and make sure you understand the concept***.

To challenge your brain to think in a new or different way, you will do horizontal learning. Horizontal learning means that when you understand a concept, you try to think about it or do it in a different way. You make a problem that is different or harder. Expample: Area of a rectangle is Length X width. You know how to do this and now do a shape that has a different shape then a rectangle.

I will use Thomas Edison quotes to think about what he thought. What do you know about Thomas Edison? Record your thoughts.

Is the first one done the smartest?

No. I believe everyone is smart in some area of Howard Gardner's intelligences. We all have a gift to give to the world. That is why I believe cooperation is so important. The reason humanity has advanced is because we can work together and learn from one another. That is what schools do for all of us. Schools teach us ideas, concepts, and thoughts. We learn to think deeper. We learn to think about how to put facts to use. Thomas Edison said, "If I could solve all the problems myself, I would."

Are you smart if you ask questions?

Yes, because you learn to think deeper by asking questions. Some of the smartest people in the area of health are asking questions about what works best to cure cancer or develop a new vaccine. If you ask enough questions, you can find the answers to most problems. Questioning is what helps us see the world around us better.

Can you learn to do things well?

Yes; the more you work on something, the better you can get at it, but remember that your brain wants to learn the things that come easiest to you, and your brain will tire more quickly when learning things that are more difficult for you to learn. That is why grit and effort will help you be successful in your learning. Thomas Edison said, "Our greatest weakness lies in giving up. The most certain way to succeed in your learning is always to try just one more time." He also said, "Genius is one percent inspiration and ninety-nine percent perspiration."

Does prior knowledge help in your understanding of concepts and the world around you?

Thomas Edison said, "I readily absorb ideas from every source, frequently starting where the last person left off." The more experiences we have, the more understanding we gain in the world around us. I hope you will try things to see what you learn from what you try. Don't let anyone tell you that you cannot be successful at something you are trying to do. If you work hard, I believe anything is possible for you!

Does trying something and failing help you in your understanding of the world?

Thomas Edison said, "Never get discouraged if you fail. Learn from it. Keep trying." Mr. Jones believes that each time you try and fail, it can be a redirect to what will work. Never quit!

Is the first student done on a test the smartest?

No, some of the smartest people will spend their lives trying to find one answer to an important question. Scientists working on the cure for cancer will spend their life on this problem. That is one of the reasons why scientists record all their thoughts and work so there is a record for other scientists to use. Scientists can use past research to help them find answers to their work.

Scientists build bridges to learn from one another by recording their thoughts and ideas.

You can do the same thing by asking teachers, students, and other people about anything you are trying to learn, to build a bridge to your understanding of concepts.

TRAINING YOUR BRAIN AND HOW IT WORKS!

You will learn more about your brain in future chapters and in upper grades, but I believe when you gain a basic understanding of how your brain works, it will help you in your learning.

The analogy I like to use is as if your brain is in a snowstorm. If the sidewalk is shoveled, you can go easily to the music store. But if you are walking to the math store and it has not been shoveled, you will need to walk and rest, and walk and rest, until you get to the math store. Over time and many walks to the math store, it is easier to get there. Your brain will always want to go back to the shoveled path going to the music store.

Our brains work this way as well. Remember when we all found out what we do best by learning about Howard Gardner's Multiple Intelligences? We all have pathways in our brains that are easier to go to. You may be music smart. The pathway for music is easier for you to learn. You like doing music. But when you are learning a math concept, the pathway has not been established for your brain. When you are working on math, you will feel tired at times. You may need to work and rest, work and rest, until you finally understand the math concept.

Effort is the key!

It's okay if you learn a concept at a different rate from others.

Our brains master different concepts at different speeds. Like an infant who falls but tries to walk again anyway, your students should be undaunted by the risk of academic failure. (Teacher: go to YouTube and show a child learning to walk to illustrate this point. Your students will see the baby fall and get up again, and it will reinforce that they need to follow that same pattern in their learning).

Almost every concept a student encounters is like walking: it's a matter of time and effort and willingness to try again in the face of temporary failure and frustration. In that sense, then, every student in every classroom can succeed. Their success is a product of their grit and determination and a teacher's ability to encourage them as they take their first wobbling "steps" in a subject. They're training their brains to keep trying until they succeed.

I had the privilege to hear Jesse Owens speak several times.
This is one of the inspiring stories he told.

As he was getting into the starting blocks to run the 100-meter race at the 1936 Olympics in Berlin, Owens noticed Glenn Cunningham, another American runner, warming up for the mile race later that day. Cunningham had been severely burned in a childhood accident. He and his brother Floyd lit a fire in their one-room schoolhouse's potbellied stove, but the fire was too close to a nearby can of kerosene. The kerosene exploded, killing Floyd and hospitalizing Glenn, who had burns over his entire body. Doctors told Cunningham he wouldn't walk again, but he tried anyway and eventually relearned how to walk. The doctors said it was a miracle, but they told him he'd never run again. He relearned how to run, too, and went on to be a five-time US champion in the 1,500 meters and a silver medalist in the 1936 Olympic games.

Owens's widespread success at those games—in front of Adolf Hitler at what was supposed to be an exhibition of German athletic prowess during Nazi Germany's swift rise to power—is legendary. Owens said that as he glanced at Cunningham, he thought, If that man can come back from all that adversity—losing his brother, getting badly burned, learning to walk, learning to run, all to become one of the greatest milers in world, I can win this 100 meters. And Owens went on to win gold in the 100 meters and three more races. Owens's message for students—for all of us, really—is that if we never give up and never quit, we can inspire each other, and ourselves, to greatness. A learned behavior can be difficult, but effort has a strong correlation to success. Desire and effort can overcome apparently insurmountable obstacles, just like they did for Glenn Cunningham. The same can be true for each and every student.

Reflect on the effort or attribute you are focused on in your learning:

How well did you do on this week's effort or attribute? How did you use the attribute or effort in your learning and in your life?

Write down the ways that the attribute you are working on has helped you in your learning and daily life. Reflecting is very helpful in gaining the attribute for lifelong use.

In a group, discuss how each of you did on your effort and how it was used in class and in your life.

Discuss with the class about this week's effort.

Remember: Effort equals greater success in your learning!
You can learn anything well with effort!

BEGINNING-OF-THE-YEAR SELF-ASSESSMENT
(for Student Only)

Student Name _____

Grade_____ School _____ Date_____

4 = Always 3 = Most of the time 2 = Sometimes 1 = Rarely 0 = Never Train your brain, don't let your brain train you!™	Your score
Achievement Through Effort: Your brain has been trained™to...	
• Believe that effort will help you be successful in obtaining your goals.	
• Believe you can fix things if they are not going well for you.	
• Stay focused on your goals.	
• Stay motivated, even when things are not going well for you.	
• Learn from your mistakes, correct the mistakes and not consider it a failure.	
• Finish all work at your best effort, never quitting.	
Safe & Respectful Environment: Your brain has been trained™to...	
• Be respectful to yourself, materials, and others.	
• Know why and how the rules help you to be successful in your learning.	
• Remember and follow the rules/directions.	
• Help others follow the rules/directions so that they can be successful.	
• Not allow bullying to take place, and if it does, you know what to do to stop it.	
• Find positive solutions during conflicts.	
Pride in Doing Your Best: Your brain has been trained™to...	
• Be eager to explore new things.	
• Come to class prepared and ready to learn.	
• Celebrate your work and the work of others.	
Interdependence: Your brain has been trained™to...	
• Adapt to different social situations.	
• Know you have the right to say respectfully what you are thinking.	
• Be a good listener and allow others to speak without interruption.	
• Work cooperatively to gain understanding of the concepts and ideas.	
• Recognize what others are doing for you and say thank you.	
• Know to go to others for support in your learning.	
• Pass it on! You help others just like they helped you.	
Responsibility for Your Learning: Your brain has been trained™to...	
• Show enthusiasm for your learning.	
• Pay attention and not get distracted by others.	
• Get to work quickly not waiting until the last minute to finish your work.	
• Ask inquiring questions to help in your learning.	
Emotional Well-Being: Your brain has been trained™to...	
• Remain calm doing what is right for yourself and others in all situations.	
• Appreciate opportunities as they come.	
• Approach new situations with excitement and positive energy.	
• Care about other people's feelings and situations (empathy).	

Totals:

MID-YEAR SELF-ASSESSMENT
(for Student and Teacher)

Student Name _____

Grade _____ **School** _____ **Date** _____

4 = Always 3 = Most of the time 2 = Sometimes 1 = Rarely 0 = Never Train your brain, don't let your brain train you!™	Your score	Teacher's score
Achievement Through Effort: Your brain has been trained™ to...		
• Believe that effort will help you be successful in obtaining your goals.		
• Believe you can fix things if they are not going well for you.		
• Stay focused on your goals.		
• Stay motivated, even when things are not going well for you.		
• Learn from your mistakes, correct the mistakes and not consider it a failure.		
• Finish all work at your best effort, never quitting.		
Safe & Respectful Environment: Your brain has been trained™ to...		
• Be respectful to yourself, materials, and others.		
• Know why and how the rules help you to be successful in your learning.		
• Remember and follow the rules/directions.		
• Help others follow the rules/directions so that they can be successful.		
• Not allow bullying to take place, and if it does, you know what to do to stop it.		
• Find positive solutions during conflicts.		
Pride in Doing Your Best: Your brain has been trained™ to...		
• Be eager to explore new things.		
• Come to class prepared and ready to learn.		
• Celebrate your work and the work of others.		
Interdependence: Your brain has been trained™ to...		
• Adapt to different social situations.		
• Know you have the right to say respectfully what you are thinking.		
• Be a good listener and allow others to speak without interruption.		
• Work cooperatively to gain understanding of the concepts and ideas.		
• Recognize what others are doing for you and say thank you.		
• Know to go to others for support in your learning.		
• Pass it on! You help others just like they helped you.		
Responsibility for Your Learning: Your brain has been trained™ to...		
• Show enthusiasm for your learning.		
• Pay attention and not get distracted by others.		
• Get to work quickly not waiting until the last minute to finish your work.		
• Ask inquiring questions to help in your learning.		
Emotional Well-Being: Your brain has been trained™ to...		
• Remain calm doing what is right for yourself and others in all situations.		
• Appreciate opportunities as they come.		
• Approach new situations with excitement and positive energy.		
• Care about other people's feelings and situations (empathy).		

Totals:

END OF YEAR-SELF-ASSESSMENT

(for Student and Teacher)

Student Name _____

Grade_____ School _____ Date_____

4 = Always 3 = Most of the time 2 = Sometimes 1 = Rarely 0 = Never Train your brain, don't let your brain train you!™	Your score	Teacher's score
Achievement Through Effort: Your brain has been trained™to…		
• Believe that effort will help you be successful in obtaining your goals.		
• Believe you can fix things if they are not going well for you.		
• Stay focused on your goals.		
• Stay motivated, even when things are not going well for you.		
• Learn from your mistakes, correct the mistakes and not consider it a failure.		
• Finish all work at your best effort, never quitting.		
Safe & Respectful Environment: Your brain has been trained™to…		
• Be respectful to yourself, materials, and others.		
• Know why and how the rules help you to be successful in your learning.		
• Remember and follow the rules/directions.		
• Help others follow the rules/directions so that they can be successful.		
• Not allow bullying to take place, and if it does, you know what to do to stop it.		
• Find positive solutions during conflicts.		
Pride in Doing Your Best: Your brain has been trained™to…		
• Be eager to explore new things.		
• Come to class prepared and ready to learn.		
• Celebrate your work and the work of others.		
Interdependence: Your brain has been trained™to…		
• Adapt to different social situations.		
• Know you have the right to say respectfully what you are thinking.		
• Be a good listener and allow others to speak without interruption.		
• Work cooperatively to gain understanding of the concepts and ideas.		
• Recognize what others are doing for you and say thank you.		
• Know to go to others for support in your learning.		
• Pass it on! You help others just like they helped you.		
Responsibility for Your Learning: Your brain has been trained™to…		
• Show enthusiasm for your learning.		
• Pay attention and not get distracted by others.		
• Get to work quickly not waiting until the last minute to finish your work.		
• Ask inquiring questions to help in your learning.		
Emotional Well-Being: Your brain has been trained™to…		
• Remain calm doing what is right for yourself and others in all situations.		
• Appreciate opportunities as they come.		
• Approach new situations with excitement and positive energy.		
• Care about other people's feelings and situations (empathy).		

Totals:

NAME ART PROJECT

1. Use a pencil and white construction paper that is 12 × 18 inches in landscape orientation and create a line that is 4 inches from the top of the paper. (The easiest way to do this is to place dots 4 inches down each edge and in the middle of the paper and connect the dots with a horizontal line.)

2. Place dots along this line and along the top edge of the paper using the following measurements:

    a. If there are 6 letters or fewer in the name, measure 3 inches between each dot and the side edges of the paper.

    b. If there are more than 6 letters in the name, measure 2 inches between each dot and the side edges of the paper.

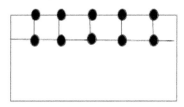

3. Connect these dots with vertical lines.

4. Make block letters within each box, making sure they touch the edge of the next box.

5. Using markers, color in the letters only. Students are encouraged to use a variety of colors and/or patterns, if desired.

6. Place a dot anywhere beneath the letters. This is the vanishing point.
7. Connect the bottom of the letters to the vanishing point.

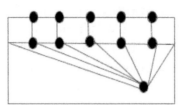

8. Draw perspective lines within letters from remaining corners.

9. Place the first letter of a color to be done between each line of the point of view.

10. Have students color between the lines of all point-of-view lines.

11. Using a black marker and a ruler, outline each letter and point-of-view line.

12. Cut out names.
13. Display the names.

ADDITIONAL INSTRUCTIONS:

You may choose to do several steps in a day, but have the students show you their work, and initial that they have done the work correctly.

Day 1: Stop to check that students have made letters correctly.

Day 2: Stop to check that all letters are colored correctly.

Day 3: Stop to check to make sure that lines are connected correctly to the bottom of the letters.

Day 4: Stop to check to make sure point-of-view lines are correct within the letters.

Day 5: Stop to check to see that all letters are placed correctly.

Possible scoring rubric:
A score of 4 (Exemplary) in the Name Art Project would be all directions completed as given with an exemplary effort. Exemplary effort with error in directions would be a score of 3.

Possible modification:
Have templates available (through step 3) for student use if they are not successful with measurements on their own.

ABOUT THOMAS EDISON

Edison had many patents in his lifetime. (Patents are legal documents that tell the world who owns the rights and money for an idea or product.) He made many products and ideas about electricity, motion pictures, and recordings.

Edison had over 1,090 US patents and as many as 2,400 patents worldwide. His patents are in every item that used electricity. He also created things like the recording industry and motion picture industry. Thomas Edison started Edison General Electric Company, now called General Electric. He invented the alkaline battery and worked to have scientist collaboration throughout the world.

Edison's life started out in a family in which his father was a railroad worker. Edison's employment started with selling newspapers and candy on a train. He read Morse code before his quest to start inventing.

You can be anything you want to be with hard work, belief in yourself, and giving your best effort!

You may choose to think about this statement almost daily!

I can be anything I want to be. I can be so much.
In order to do this, I must create good habits!

This means: train your brain, don't let your brain train you!
You do the hard work, and never let your brain tell you to give up or that you can't do something. You have trained your brain to know, and you believe you can accomplish anything!

***Look at these Thomas Edison quotes and write down
what you think they mean on the next page.***

Then discuss with your group or class.

- "Genius is one percent inspiration and ninety-nine percent perspiration."

- "Opportunity is missed by most people because it is dressed in overalls and looks like work."

- "When you have exhausted all possibilities, remember you haven't."

- "If we did all the things we are capable of, we would literally astonish ourselves."

- "Our greatest weakness is giving up. The most certain way to succeed is always to try one more time."

- "I have not failed. I just found ten thousand ways that did not work."

- "Nearly every man who develops an idea works up to a point where it looks impossible and then he gets discouraged. That is not the place to get discouraged."

- "The chief function of the body is to carry the brain around."

- "The value of an idea lies in using it."

"Genius is one percent inspiration and ninety-nine percent perspiration."

I believe Edison is saying most of a person's success is in hard work because after you have an idea, you will need to work hard to make it become a reality. I like this statement: "Champions are no different from you or I. The only difference is they act upon their dreams." I want each of you to be a champion by always acting on your dreams.

"Opportunity is missed by most people because it is dressed in overalls and looks like work."

Many people do not succeed in life not because they cannot do something but because they do not do the work it takes for it to happen for them.

"When you have exhausted all possibilities, remember you haven't."

What this is saying to me is that when you think you have done everything you can to make something happen, do even more.

My PIL (partner in life), JoJo, and I wanted to have a three-season patio in our condo. The association said we could not have windows because it would reflect and look different from all the screened-in patios. I was told by a board member "not to get my hopes up on the board approving the project." I told her, "I always have my hopes up!" JoJo and I worked on taking pictures of all the screened-in patios. The picture showed any differences in the screens. We also answered all the board members' concerns about a sprinkler system, reflection of glass, and so on. We then wrote a letter to each board member with all this information. The Board approved our project! Always keep your hopes up!

Remember to do everything you can in a respectful way to get your needs met. All of our voices have value. If we listen to one another, we will learn and know much more about our world.

"If we did all the things we are capable of, we would literally astonish ourselves."

If we work hard and think deep about the world around us, especially in the areas we are most talented in, we can be amazing. For each of us, the amazing will be in different areas. Some of you may like working with your hands and be great mechanics, landscapers, painters, plumbers, electricians, and many other choices. Others of you may be doctors, lawyers, teachers, engineers, and many other professions. The point is to never give up and you will find you're amazing!

"Our greatest weakness is giving up. The most certain way to succeed is always to try one more time."

Many people give up too soon and never see what could have been.

"I have not failed. I just found ten thousand ways that did not work."

Sometimes we discover something different from what we are looking for if we keep trying. Penicillin is a great example of this. It was a complete accident that it was discovered. Alexander Fleming, who is credited with the discovery of penicillin, said, "One sometimes finds what one is not looking for. When I woke up just after dawn on September 28, 1928, I certainly didn't plan to revolutionize all medicine by discovering the world's first antibiotic, or bacteria killer. But I guess that was exactly what I did."

I believe that if you learn from a mistake, it is a lesson, not a failure. The more we try different things and ideas, the more we learn about ourselves and about the world around us. Learn to believe in yourself and your thinking as you listen to others' ideas. Do not be afraid to say what you think! You ALWAYS have the right to speak your truth!

"Nearly every man who develops an idea works up to a point where it looks impossible and then he gets discouraged. That is not the place to get discouraged."

Nearly every person who develops and idea will work very hard on the idea. They may become discouraged. REMEMBER, "Do not become discouraged but rather keep yourself encouraged."

"The chief function of the body is to carry the brain around."

The brain is the most important part of your body; that is why I say, "Train your brain, don't let your brain train you."

"The value of an idea lies in using it."

You need to act on your ideas and dreams or they never become your reality!

SECTION II:
THE IMPORTANCE OF COMMUNICATING YOUR IDEAS IN POSITIVE WAYS

Dear Mr. Jones,

Thank-you for everything you did for me and others. I think you are a great teacher because you never get mad at us and understand us. Please don't retire because lots of 4th graders want you as a teacher next year. I will never forget your really funny jokes and riddles you told us. Thank you for everything.

Sincerly

Diana - 231

Hi Mr. Jones! It's me Chantell! I think your a great teacher because you incourage us to be the best learners we can be! You always say Bee happy! I will most of the time! I'm kinda sad because your retriring and I haven't got to know you for a while. But I'll always Remember you!!"

From: Chantell.

Dear MR. Jones

I think you are a great teacher, because you help me learn alot.

You give me work that challenges me while being funny and having fun.

I love your saying train your brain

I will remember your jokes your dancing, and your "wonderful" singing

I have grown so much as a student. I have learned so much and I hope you have a great retirement

from: Gavin

Accountability Talk

Learn to use ***accountable talk*** with one another! Accountable talk is *accountability to the learning community, to accurate knowledge and to rigorous thinking*. When you talk in this form, you are working together to solve a problem in a positive way. Agreement, disagreement, clarification, confusion, and extension are the areas where accountable talk is helpful.

When you are discussing a topic, try to work on the skill of accountable talk. It will help you to talk about the topic and not about the person. The people you are working with will be more open to your ideas and feel less threatened by your thoughts.

It is also helpful to talk to students about specific words and phrases that allow them to talk and disagree with each other in a respectful manner, known as *accountable talk*. I learned about "accountable talk" as the lead for my school in the IFL initiative. Here are some examples:

For example:

Someone is talking about how to find the area of a rectangle and you do not understand it. You may say, "I don't understand the area of a rectangle. Can you show me in a different way how to find it?" You may say, "I am confused about this concept. Please say more about this." Then the discussion is about the concept, not about the person. Don't say, "You aren't explaining this concept very well!" Make your statement about the problem, not about the person!

Agreement:
"I agree with ____ because . . ."
"I like what ____ said because . . ."

Disagreement:
"I disagree because . . ."
"I push back on that because . . ."

Clarification:
"Please repeat that."
"What I heard was ____. Could you explain that more, please?"
"Would you say more about that?"
"Could you state the evidence or source, please?"

Confirmation:
"I like the way you said ____.
I agree because ____."
Or "I'd like to add on to that statement by saying ____."

Confusion:
"I don't understand ____."
"I am confused about ____."

Extension:
"I am wondering what if ____."
"I would like to know more about ____."
"This makes me think of ____."
"Can you tell me more about ____."

FOUR CLASSIC VIRTUES

Let us look at the best we can be through the view of the four classic virtues.

WISDOM

Knowledge and the search for what is fact.

COURAGE

Having the will to do what is best even when we are afraid or we desire what is less than ideal.

MODERATION

Letting our intellect and our spiritual side rule over our desires.

JUSTICE

A balanced and proportional life for ourselves and others around us.

Write down what you think each of the Four VIrtues mean to you.

Give examples if that will help you explain your thinking.

WISDOM

This is looking for facts about your thoughts and ideas in the world and of the world. When you talk about a topic, you try to support your fact with many sources. This is important because there are some people that try to manipulate your thinking. The main ways to manipulate your thinking are fear, nationalism, superiority, or loyalty.

> **Example**: You have a friend who tells you not to like someone named Jim. They say, "If you're my friend, you won't talk to Jim." (Loyalty) They could say, "If you talk to Jim, I will tell everyone not to like you." (Fear) They may say, "I know you are better than Jim and smarter than Jim. Let's not talk to him." (Superiority) And finally, "We are English-speaking people, so let's not talk to Jim, because he speaks Spanish." (Nationalism.)

COURAGE

It is hard to do the right thing at times. We may want to do something that we know is not good for us. It may be done out of fear or make us feel better about ourselves at the expense of others.

> **Your response is, "I will not hurt someone to gain your favor! I believe we need to all work together."** This shows courage, because you had to say something against your friend's thoughts but you did the most positive thing anyway. This is hard to do for many people.

Write your thoughts about the Four Classic Virtues below:

Discuss your list with the students around you, and add any new ideas to your list.

Next, with your teacher, discuss as a class, and add any additional ideas to your list.

MODERATION

Our brains create different emotions and needs to make us feel better about ourselves. This can be done in a positive way or in a negative way. Some of these emotions or needs are the following: anger, fear, shame, cruelty, envy, jealousy, power, control, importance, admiration, adoration, appreciation, anxiety, boredom, awkwardness, confusion, calmness, disgust, empathy, excitement, interest, horror, nostalgia, relief, success, wealth, joy, sadness, romance, satisfaction, surprise, desire, and happiness. In your lifetime you will make millions of decisions. It will be a change to always make the most positive decisions. When you see your decision is not good for you or others you can learn from that decision and understand how to make a better decision next time. Prior knowledge is very powerful, so the more you experience and learn the more you can understand.

> **Example**: Anger—both energies. I believe it can be both because if someone hits my friend, I would have a right to be angry, but what I do with that anger is important. If I stopped the fight and let others know it is harmful to both people, that would be positive energy. If I started to call the person names, hit them, or hate them, that would be negative. You can hate the behavior but not the person.

How does it hurt both people? When you are an adult, if you hit someone, that is assault and you may go to jail for that. The person that is hitting your friends needs to learn self-control. If they get angry, how can they control it, and how can they tell the person what they want to happen? Of course, the person being hit will also get hurt.

You may have read about men fighting each other. The person getting hit falls, hits his head, and later dies. The man that hit the other person is charged with manslaughter and goes to prison. Both people are harmed. That is what negative energy does! I believe it always harms everyone involved!

JUSTICE

You believe in fairness, truth, honesty, and kindness with personal strength. You have empathy for self and others. You reflect on how to improve yourself and the world at large. You want consequences for yourself and others when they do wrong, not to harm them but to help them learn to be a better person for themselves and the community as a whole by balancing what they do in life.

> **Example one**: If we eat a balanced diet, we stay well and healthy, but if we eat too much sugar, salt, fat, meat, or food in general, it can harm us.

> **Example two**: If we exercise in balance, it will be good for our hearts and circulation, but if we exercise too much, it can cause damage to our muscles or joints.

> **Example three**: If we watch TV, we can learn about the world and be more aware of what is happening in the world, but if we watch too much TV, it may harm our eyes, cause us to lose sleep, or take time away from our friends.

Can you write down any other examples of having balance in our lives?

Discuss your list with the students around you and add any new ideas to your list.

Next, with your teacher, discuss as a class, and add any additional ideas to your list.

You may believe good positive energy will not let others control us. We will see through the people that are trying to trick us. We will remember positive energy is loving, strong, supportive, joyful, caring, truthful, respectful, appreciative of others' gifts, listening to our and others' truths. Positive energy is done so everyone can see it.

Reflect on each of these emotions and decide if the emotion is positive, negative, or both, and then write why you believe your answer is correct.

Example: Anger—both emotions, because if you are angry about someone doing something harmful, it would be positive for you to stop the harm with your voice, ideas, or statements. If you harmed someone because you are angry, it is a negative energy.

Now you do the rest of the words from left to right on the following page.
(ex: Fear, then Shame, and so on.)

Anger	Fear	Shame	Cruelty
Envy	Jealousy	Power	Control
Importance	Admiration	Adoration	Appreciation
Anxiety	Boredom	Awkwardness	Confusion
Calmness	Disgust	Empathy	Excitement
Interest	Horror	Nostalgia	Relief
Success	Wealth	Joy	Sadness
Romance	Satisfaction	Surprise	Desire
Happiness	Greed		

Bloom's Taxonomy

I think it will be helpful for you to know the different levels of learning because the more you learn in the higher level, the greater your understanding of the concepts you are learning.

Benjamin Bloom created the **different levels of thinking** from least to greatest knowledge and understanding.

- Knowing
- Understanding
- Applying
- Analyzing
- Creating
- Evaluating

There are **three main domains** of learning to know about and use to learn at the highest levels

- **Cognitive** (thinking)
- **Affective** (social/emotional/feeling)
- **Psychomotor** (physical/kinesthetic)

Each domain has a taxonomy—a classification—associated with it.

For example, if we were to use the United States of America as the topic, this is what it would look like:

Knowing:
What are the names of the fifty states and their capitals?

Understanding:
How do you think the United States became a country, and why did its people want a new country?

Applying:
You are going to the state of Minnesota. Where do you think you would stop to see the capitol building, and why do you think that?

Analyzing:
Are there any laws that you feel help all of us be more successful in our lives? Why?

Creating:
What new laws would be helpful to all of us in having a more perfect union, and why?

Evaluating:
Is our country doing a good job of keeping our republic strong and working for all of us?

Use Bloom's taxonomy in your learning. Each time you are learning something new, think about which one of Bloom's taxonomies you are using.

Remember: you can learn anything with effort!

EXAMPLE OF STUDENT-EFFORT JOURNALS

Q1 Week 4 October 3-7
4=Always   3= Most of the time   2= Sometimes   1= Rarely   0= Never

In all my middle school classes this week:

5	I am a responsible and focused student.	1	2	③	4
6	My brain makes respectful choices	1	2	③	4
7	I put time and effort into class and homework.	1	②	3	4
8	I am a positive class citizen	1	2	③	4

This Week

D   What went well this week in my learning?

Studied homework that I didn't understand and worked on it till I understood.

E   What could've gone even better in my learning?

I could've worked on homework for longer instead of procrasinating.

F   How do I get there?

Put phone away and don't procrasinate.

SECTION III: LEARNING CRITICAL THINKING SKILLS WITH INFORMATION AND TECHNOLOGY

Dear: Mr. Jones,

You were the best teacher I ever had
You showed me what teachers do
You showed me that teachers can
be like your own parents they always
want you to do the right thing or choice
and You made me feel like my own
Father, thank you for this wonderful
Year and I'm going to remember this
for ever and Yes, this was a great experience
for me, I thank you for it again, I'll
miss you a lot, I hope You'll have a great
life, and let's keep in contect on e-mail.

Thank
You

Dear Mr. Jones,
you are a sensational teacher
because you make learning fun
not boring. when you tell the
hard riddles, I get flabergested
because of the answer. I even
like your singing (scream style). I
well miss you very much, I hope
you can read the book I will publish,
is called "Search for the stone and
the Heros". Sincerely Abdulwahid

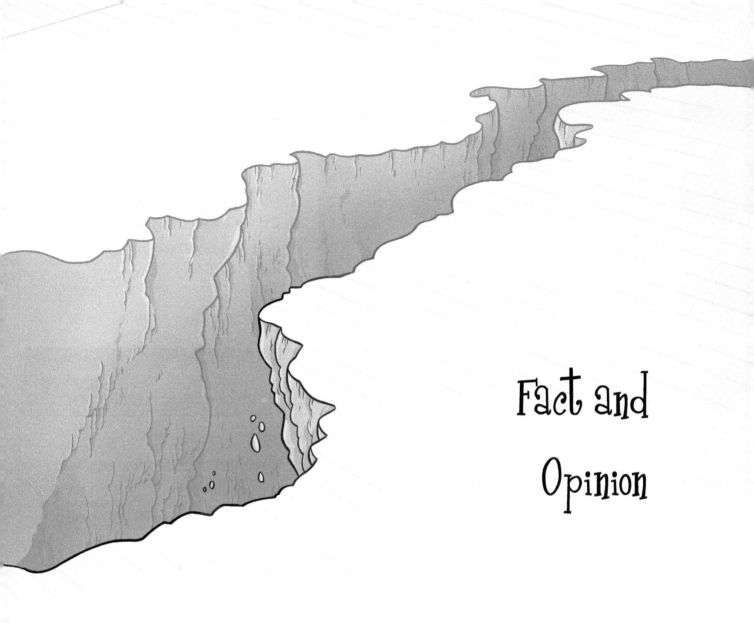

Fact and Opinion

Your world will be different from any time in history because there will be technology to trick you into believing the unbelievable. The internet will have information on its sites that appears to be from someone you trust, and it may be from another country. If you learn to train your brain and not let your brain train you, you will figure out what is true and what is a lie. **USE the parts of your knowledge to create a factual bridge to the world we live in.**

We will now look at the ways you can train your brain to know what is fact and what is opinion. There is a lot to do to train your brain to do careful thinking. Your thinking is created by your experiences, genetics, parenting, where and when you are born, and world events of your time.

When writing an article or evaluating different topics, we will use the *5 Ws and How,* to guide your thinking. I will give you the areas of thought, and then we can practice using these skills to train your brain to make good decisions.

Who

- Will this help?
- Will this harm?
- Will this affect the most?
- Will this most benefit?
- Would be a good person to ask about this?
- Was the first person to think this?
- Has proved this with facts?
- Made the decision about this?

When

- Would this benefit our society?
- Would this cause a problem?
- Is the best time to implement this?
- Do we ask for support on this?
- Do we expect this to happen?
- Will we know we have been successful?

What

- Would be an alternative or different perspective?
- Would an opposite (counter) argument be?
- Would be the best or worst outcome?
- Is the most or least important part?
- Can be done to make this a positive outcome?
- Is getting in the way?
- **Are the strengths and weakness of this perspective?**

Why

- Is this a problem?
- Is there a need to change this?
- Is this relevant?
- Are we influenced by this person or idea?
- Should we know about this?
- Has it been done this way in the past?
- Have we allowed this to happen?

Where

- Did this idea, concept, or situation originate?
- Are there similar ideas, concepts, or situations?
- Can we get more information about this topic?
- Do we go for help?
- Does this idea take us?
- Can we improve this idea?

How

- Is this a problem?
- Is this a disruption to something?
- Do we approach this?
- Does this benefit us?
- Could this harm us?
- Could we change this for our own good?

Some people want you to believe things so they will get something from you. They may say something to make you angry or make you feel that your decision must be made right away. They do this because they know if they get you angry, the pathways in your brain will not work as well, and if you don't get time to think through things, you are more likely to make a mistake in your thinking.

Example: Someone you like (Betty) tells you that another friend (Sara) is talking about you in a bad way. This would make most of us angry. You may not stop to use the 5 W's and How. You could just go over and yell at your friend Sara. Betty may be telling the truth, but she may also be lying about this. Betty may be lying because she is mad at Sara and would like to hurt Sara. She is using you to hurt Sara.

If you used the 5W's and How, it might look like this. Betty, when did Sara say this? Did anyone else hear Betty say it? Why would Betty say this? I will ask Betty about this and hear what she says happened.

Example: A person you like, Jim, says to you that Tim took a new watch from him. So you and several of your friends go and take the watch away from Tim. Can Jim tell you the following using the 5 W's and How?

- Who saw the watch being taken?
- What kind of watch is it?
- Where was the watch taken?
- When was the watch taken? Why was the watch taken from Jim?

When we are angry about something we see as unfair, our brains many times do not stop to think about the 5 W's and How.

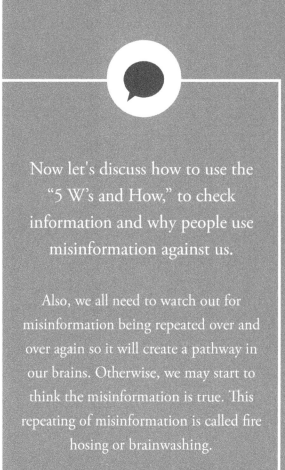

Now let's discuss how to use the "5 W's and How," to check information and why people use misinformation against us.

Also, we all need to watch out for misinformation being repeated over and over again so it will create a pathway in our brains. Otherwise, we may start to think the misinformation is true. This repeating of misinformation is called fire hosing or brainwashing.

Remember our discussion about pathways. Once a pathway is formed in our brains, our brains want to go back to that idea or belief. This is like the example of the snowstorm discussion on page 46. We are able to walk where the path has been shoveled for us. That is the way we want to go because it is easiest for us to walk, but it may not be the safest way or the right way.

Please write your own example in your journal about an experience you may have had and discuss in groups or as a class using the 5 W's and How.

Each of you can find a topic to use this method, but first, let us try one more together.

Your friend says, "I read the earth is not a sphere. It is flat."

How do you disprove this information using the 5 W's and How?

Discuss the above statement as a room or in groups.

WE WILL LOOK AT FACT OR OPINION.

After each statement, write F for Fact or O for Opinion, and why you think that way. Record your thoughts in a journal.

1.   Everyone is nice.

2.   The world is a sphere.

3.   I am good at math.

4.   I can be good at math.

5.   The best color in the world is green.

6.   All cars are safe.

7.   The best food to eat is pizza.

8.   Dogs are a man's best friend.

9.   The truth always comes out.

10. $10 \times 4 = 40$

11. The world is getting warmer.

12. The capital of Minnesota is St. Paul.

13. The greatest president is George Washington.

14. Sunlight is important for plants to grow.

15. What goes up must come down.

16. There are twenty-four hours in a day.

17. $5(2 \times 5 - 3) = 35$

18. The USA has an election for its president every four years.

19. The three primary colors are red, yellow, and blue.

20. Smart people are good spellers.

*My thinking on why each of the topics is **Fact or Opinion** is below.*

See if you agree with me or not. You can add your own ideas to the list that has been suggested below.

1. **Everyone is nice.**

   Opinion: There are many factors to being a nice person, like what behaviors people have learned from those around them, such as their friends or parents.

2. **The world is a sphere.**

   Fact: We have equipment (satellites and space stations) that will take pictures of our planet to prove it is a sphere.

3. **I am good at math.**

   Fact and Opinion: We can be very knowledgeable in one area of math and still learning in other areas of math. Math is a general term, not a specific topic. For example: area is one main concept you may understand well, and slope may be an area you are still working to understand.

4. **I can be good at math.**

   Fact and Opinion: You may have to work very hard to understand multiplication and not understand the topic of square roots. If we work hard and put in great effort, my belief is we can learn any concept in math.

5. **The best color in the world is green.**

   Opinion: Each of us have opinions of what colors we like.

6. **All cars are safe.**

   Fact and Opinion: Manufacturers continue to design cars to improve safety, but we still have car crashes and people dying. So cars are not totally safe.

7. **The best food to eat is pizza.**

   Opinion: We all have an opinion on which food we like best.

8. **Dogs are a man's best friend.**

   Opinion: This can be true for some people, but others like cats. "Dogs are a woman's best friend" can also be true!

9. **The truth always comes out**

   Opinion: The truth may be hidden from us by others.

10. **10 × 4 = 40**

    Fact: This is always true.

11. **The world is getting warmer.**

    Fact: Scientists measure the temperature of the entire planet; this is called climate. If you are talking about temperature in a specific place on the planet at a specific time, it is called weather.

12. **The capital of Minnesota is St. Paul.**

    Fact: The state of Minnesota's capital is indeed St. Paul!

13. **The greatest president is George Washington.**

    Opinion: We all may pick different presidents as the best. We all may have different ideas of what characteristics make a good president.

14. Sunlight is important for plants to grow.

Fact: Plants cannot grow without light. Photosynthesis is plants changing light energy into chemical energy. Humans and animals eat the plants, and then the plants are changed into energy by our bodies.

15. What goes up must come down.

Fact or Opinion: It is a fact if on Earth because of gravity, but if you are in a vacuum, like in space, objects do not come down.

16. There are 24 hours in a day

Fact: We use a twenty-four-hour clock on Earth.

17. 5(2 × 5 - 3) = 35

Fact: This is a math equation.

18. The USA has an election for its president every four years.

Fact: This is what our system of government has agreed to do.

19. The three primary colors are: red, yellow, and blue!

Fact: If you mix these colors, you can create all the other colors we have.

20. Smart people are good spellers.

Opinion: As we have discussed, all of us have different attributes that make us smart. The ability to spell well is one of many qualities that a person can have.

The author of this book is an example of someone learning something that at one time he was not good at. He was knowledgeable in math and science in high school and was not a good writer or reader. He needed to become a good writer to share his ideas and thoughts about learning with other people. He asked for help from people who are great writers or editors and took that knowledge to become a better writer myself. He loved learning, so he kept reading and reading to gain the understanding and in that process gained a larger vocabulary. Later in life as an educator, he found out that he had dyslexia (the numbers or letters may be reversed as he reads). He shows his belief that anyone can become good at something if they work at it and spend the time needed to improve.

All of you can get any skill with hard work and support from others. You deserve to do this for your success in your life and your learning!

Now we will use the information on critical thinking to assess some information.

Remember to go through the 5 Ws and How! Please record your thoughts below or in your journal.

Who makes a good leader in your belief system, and why?

Your thoughts:

Cooperative group thoughts:

Class thoughts:

What would make world peace possible?

Your thoughts:

Cooperative group thoughts:

Class thoughts:

How does a person almost always get their homework done correctly and on time?

Your thoughts:

Cooperative group thoughts:

Class thoughts:

How do we make friends and keep them?

Your thoughts:

Cooperative group thoughts:

Class thoughts:

What does social justice look like to you?

Your thoughts:

Cooperative group thoughts:

Class thoughts:

Why do some people seem to learn math faster than other people?

Your thoughts:

Cooperative group thoughts:

Class thoughts:

Why are cooperative people successful?

Your thoughts:

Cooperative group thoughts:

Class thoughts:

Why do some people seem to be harder workers than other people?

Your thoughts:

Cooperative group thoughts:

Class thoughts:

How do we learn to do something well?

Your thoughts:

Cooperative group thoughts:

Class thoughts:

Can people be racist, and can there be institutional racism?

Your thoughts:

Cooperative group thoughts:

Class thoughts:

You and your teacher work to create a topic to think about and discuss.
Record your thoughts in your journal.

My thoughts on each of the questions you have discussed.

We are working to help all of us have the tools we need to bridge what is true and what is misinformation or false. We all have a right to our opinions, and we can listen using accountable talk, as we learned earlier in this book.

Who makes a good leader in your belief system, and why?

A good leader shows us positive energy. They treat all of us respectfully. They know if someone disagrees with them, it is okay to have a difference of opinion. They have empathy for others, listen to others' ideas, and then act decisively. They work cooperatively with all. They ask others that have an expertise in an area that they are working on for help. They try to improve on who they are and are truthful all of the time. You can trust them.

What would make world peace possible?

Cooperation is the most important attribute to world peace. If all countries worked together for the common good for all humans, we could have world peace. This is very difficult because there are so many leaders who have their own faults in their personalities. Remember, some leaders are looking for power, fame, or glory, and they are not there to do what is best for the community they lead. I often think of the phrase survival of the fittest. Many people think that it is the strongest who survive, but many scientists believe that it is the most cooperative who survive. The people who can work together will be more likely to survive.

One example of this is *a dog*. Dogs were at one time wolves, and one pack of wolves made friends with humans. Dogs now are fed, sheltered, and protected by humans. My opinion is the dogs have a good life and live longer than wolves do.

How does a person almost always get their homework done correctly and on time?

The person knows "effort equals better outcomes." They ask a lot of questions, and they find people who know how to do the homework. They keep asking questions until they are sure they know how to do the homework. They have a great understanding of the homework.

We can learn anything if we are willing to put the time and effort into the learning! Remember how the baby learned to walk. (We also know if we have a disability, it will be more challenging for us.)

How do we make friends and keep them?

We look for people we can trust and watch how they treat other people. If they are mean or dishonest to others, they can do that to us, so I am very careful if I see them doing these things to others. I meet healthy people if I am doing healthy things. We do fun things together and stay healthy together.

What does social justice look like to you?

Social justice is when no one is above the law, when we are all treated equally.

Why do some people seem to learn math faster than other people?

If the person is logic smart, they will have a brain pathway that makes it easier for them to learn math concepts. If we have a different brain pathway—say, in music—then we will have to work harder to create the pathway in math concepts. Remember how babies learn to walk. It is okay to fall down—just get back up and try again.

Why are cooperative people successful?

Cooperative people can use one another's strengths to complete a task. They trust one another to do their part for the greater good of the team.

Why do some people seem to be harder workers than other people?

Some people may work harder than others. This may have to do with many factors: genetics, parenting, more opportunity for experiences (prior knowledge), training of their brains to know effort equates to better outcomes.

How do we learn to do something well?

We learn to do things well by having the tools we have talked about: our effort, the belief we can learn anything, finding people with the knowledge to help us succeed in what we want to do well, learning from our mistakes, and doing things differently after our mistakes.

Can people be racist, and can there be institutional racism?

Some people are racist! They believe they are better than a different race. This is called being biased. People can be biased about many different things—believing, for example, that women can't run a marathon well, Asians are smarter in math than other people, Black people can run faster than other people, Native Americans care more about our environment than others do. All these statements and many more like them are called generalizations. A generalization is putting all the people of an ethnicity or gender into a group.

Example: All Asians are great in math. We know from our discussion of Howard Gardner's Multiple Intelligences that we all have pathways that are easier or harder for us. The belief that one race is better is not factually true. That belief limits us on what we can do or what we can be.

People that are white supremacists think that they are better than all other races. This cannot be true, because the only difference in the color of someone's skin is the melanin in our skin. Melanin will darken our skin if we are in a sunny area of the world over many years; then our skin will be darkened at birth to protect us from too much sun. Nature is amazing!

You or your teacher work to create a topic to think about and discuss it together.

Remember: We all have talents to share with ourselves and other people!

RESOLVING CONFLICTS!

To resolve a conflict or to address being disrespected, there are four things to say.

1. **This is what you did that I did not like.**

2. **This is how it made me feel.**

3. **This is what I would like you to do.**

4. **This is what I will do if you do not stop.**

Example: Someone is calling you names on the playground. You would say something like this: "You are calling me names. It is making me feel sad. Please stop. And if you do not stop, I will let the playground supervisor know what you are doing."

We are letting the person know that what they are doing is not okay. We are also telling on them to stop their behavior. It is harmful to you but also harmful to them. We are not telling on them to get them in trouble; we are telling on them to help them become a better person. The person learns how to express their feelings instead of calling you a name. Maybe they wanted you to do something with them. They did not know how to express this in words, so they called you a name.

I believe it is important to stand up to a bully as they are insecure inside. One book that discusses bullying is Secret of the Peaceful Warrior by Dan Millman.

I believe in restitution. Diane Gossen has a book on this approach. The approach is as follows: The student who calls you a name would say, "This is what I did wrong, this is what I will do to make this up to you, and this is what I will do next time."

Example: "I was calling you a name, I am sorry for calling you a name, and next time, I will tell you why I am mad at you."

Students and teachers, please practice these skills as you have conflicts in your class.

Students - give an example of something or someone who has harmed you in some way. Remember not to use the names of the people. We are learning to use our new skills and naming the people who get in the way of our learning these skills.

Write your example below:

Discuss in a group, how to say your example using the four steps:

"This is what you did, this is how it made me feel, this is what I would like you to do, and this is what I will do if your behavior does not change."

The Restitution: What would the person say in their restitution of this situation?

HOW TO BE A GOOD LISTENER:

1. Listen to what the person is saying with eye contact when you can.

2. Repeat what you heard, using accountable talk.

> Example: Your friend says she is mad at another person, Terry, because she has not called.
>
> You say, "What I hear you saying is you are upset with Terry because she has not called you. It sounds like you would like her to call? Can I give you some suggestions on what to do?"

Share your thoughts about problems you are having. Listen to one another, and practice active listening.

Write your example below:

Discuss strategies for how to listen to the problem using accountable talk:

Discuss ideas with your class about how to listen and solve the problem using accountable talk:

The Story of the Little Boy and the Wolves

The little boy went to his grandfather, who was the chief of the tribe, and asked, "Grandfather, why is it I think of doing the wrong thing or the thing I know is bad for me or other people?"

Grandfather said to the boy, "There are two wolves within you, and they are fighting over you. One wants you to do what is right for you, and one wants you to do what will harm you and other people."

The boy then asked,
"Grandfather, which wolf will get me?"

Grandfather said, " The one you feed."

I hope all of you feed your best selves and make the world a better place for all of us.

FREQUENTLY USED STATEMENTS

Use the following statements with your class as much as possible to create a strong and positive energy in your room.

"I" Statements
- I believe if you give your best effort, you'll be successful in this class.
- I want what's best for you.
- I want to meet your needs.
- I believe in respect for you and others.
- I love to learn, and I want to hear from each of you so I have a greater understanding of your thinking.
- I know you can learn this with support from others and from me.
- I want you to think at as a deep a level as you can.
- I want you to know your voice and ideas have value to me and to many others in this class.
- I'm not disappointed in you; I'm disappointed in your behavior.
- I want you to succeed in your learning. That's why I am asking you to _____.
- I believe you deserve to have a great life. That's why I am asking you to _____.

"We" Statements
- We believe all of us can learn.
- We learn by listening to each other's thoughts.
- We believe that if we give our best effort, we'll have our best outcomes.
- We believe in respecting everyone.
- We believe no one can disrespect us or anyone else.
- We believe we have a right to state our thoughts and feelings.
- We believe we deserve to be heard by others.
- We believe everything we do is to help each other grow into the best people we can be.

"We Agreed" Statements
- We all agreed to work with our best effort. It's not fair to the group when you're talking instead of listening to what others say.
- We agreed to this idea: Train your brain, don't let your brain train you.

Student's Self-Assessment

Student Name _____

Grade_____ **School** _____ **Date**_____

4 = Always 3 = Most of the time 2 = Sometimes 1 = Rarely 0 = Never Train your brain, don't let your brain train you!™	Your score	Teacher's score
Achievement Through Effort: Your brain has been trained™to...		
• Believe that effort will help you be successful in obtaining your goals.		
• Believe you can fix things if they are not going well for you.		
• Stay focused on your goals.		
• Stay motivated, even when things are not going well for you.		
• Learn from your mistakes, correct the mistakes and not consider it a failure.		
• Finish all work at your best effort, never quitting.		
Safe & Respectful Environment: Your brain has been trained™to...		
• Be respectful to yourself, materials, and others.		
• Know why and how the rules help you to be successful in your learning.		
• Remember and follow the rules/directions.		
• Help others follow the rules/directions so that they can be successful.		
• Not allow bullying to take place, and if it does, you know what to do to stop it.		
• Find positive solutions during conflicts.		
Pride in Doing Your Best: Your brain has been trained™to...		
• Be eager to explore new things.		
• Come to class prepared and ready to learn.		
• Celebrate your work and the work of others.		
Interdependence: Your brain has been trained™to...		
• Adapt to different social situations.		
• Know you have the right to say respectfully what you are thinking.		
• Be a good listener and allow others to speak without interruption.		
• Work cooperatively to gain understanding of the concepts and ideas.		
• Recognize what others are doing for you and say thank you.		
• Know to go to others for support in your learning.		
• Pass it on! You help others just like they helped you.		
Responsibility for Your Learning: Your brain has been trained™to...		
• Show enthusiasm for your learning.		
• Pay attention and not get distracted by others.		
• Get to work quickly not waiting until the last minute to finish your work.		
• Ask inquiring questions to help in your learning.		
Emotional Well-Being: Your brain has been trained™to...		
• Remain calm doing what is right for yourself and others in all situations.		
• Appreciate opportunities as they come.		
• Approach new situations with excitement and positive energy.		
• Care about other people's feelings and situations (empathy).		

Totals:

Student's Daily Self-Assessment

Student Name:_____ Advisory: _____

Grade: _____   Date from: _____ to: _____

Train your brain, don't let your brain train you™

Scoring:	7 - 8	5 - 6	3 - 4	1 - 2	0
	Always	Most of the Time	Sometimes	Rarely	Never

Attribute I am working on: _____

X = *In my seat on time with materials needed for my class out and ready.*

Class Period	Monday		Tuesday		Wednesday		Thursday		Friday	
Hour 1										
Hour 2										
Hour 3										
Hour 4										
Hour 5										
Hour 6										
Hour 7										
Advisory										

Self-Reflection

What I did to train my brain this week: _____

_____

_____

Parent Signature: _____

9/7/16

My top five qualities for an exemplary students are- listens to the teacher because if you don't listen to the teacher you will not learn anything. Takes notes because if you take notes you'll be able to study them over and over until you actually understand

Q1 Week 1: August 29 to September 2
4=Always   3= Most of the time   2= Sometimes 1= Rarely   0= Never

In all my middle school classes this week:

1	I am a responsible and focused student.	1	2	3	(4)
2	My brain makes respectful choices	1	2	(3)	4
3	I put time and effort into class and homework.	1	2	(3)	4
4	I am a positive class citizen	1	2	(3)	4

This Week

A.	What went well this week in my learning?
	I did well on the worksheets I got
B	What could've gone even better in my learning?
	focused more
C	How do I get there?
	don't talk and pay attention.

A positive school attitude is hard working, happy faces, and you should feel like you understand what your learning.

Q1 Week 3: September 26-30
4=Always   3= Most of the time   2= Sometimes   1= Rarely   0= Never

In all my middle school classes this week:

5	I am a responsible and focused student.	1	2	③	4
6	My brain makes respectful choices	1	②	3	4
7	I put time and effort into class and homework.	1	2	③	4
8	I am a positive class citizen	1	2	③	4

This Week

D	What went well this week in my learning?
	I listened in most classes

E	What could've gone even better in my learning?
	I could have paid more attention.

F	How do I get there?
	Not talk as much

121

EFFORT-SCORING IDEAS CREATED BY EDUCATION2ASPIRE-TRAINED TEACHERS

Here are some of the various ideas used by teachers in recording their students' effort grades and reflections on Education2Aspire attributes.

Name _____ Date_____

Advisory Monthly Review

1. What score (4-1) do you give yourself for all your classes the month in the following categories? Circle the appropriate score for each.

I was prepared for class (focus)	4 3 2 1
I was focused and on task (focus and self-control)	4 3 2 1
I was polite and respectful (social skills)	4 3 2 1
I asked questions (focus and social skills)	4 3 2 1
I actively participated (focus and social skills)	4 3 2 1
I had a positive attitude about learning and stuck with it (perseverance)	4 3 2 1

2. How did your perseverance, focus, self-control, and social skills in the past month affect **your learning**?

3. How did your perseverance, focus, self-control, and social skills in the past month affect **your academic performance** - your grades?

"Student Weekly Effort Chart"

4=All Classroom Expectations Followed
3=Most Classroom Expectations Followed (missed 1 or 2)
2=Some Classroom Expectations Followed (class timeout)
1=Little to No Classroom Expectations Followed (buddy room, etc.)

Week Of:_____

Name	Mon.	Tues.	Wed.	Thur.	Fri.
Note:					

"Student Weekly Effort Chart"

4=All Classroom Expectations Followed
3=Most Classroom Expectations Followed (missed 1 or 2)
2=Some Classroom Expectations Followed (class timeout)
1=Little to No Classroom Expectations Followed (buddy room, etc.)

Week Of:_____

Name	Mon.	Tues.	Wed.	Thur.	Fri.
Note:					

"Student Weekly Effort Chart"

4=All Classroom Expectations Followed
3=Most Classroom Expectations Followed (missed 1 or 2)
2=Some Classroom Expectations Followed (class timeout)
1=Little to No Classroom Expectations Followed (buddy room, etc.)

Week Of:_____

Name	Mon.	Tues.	Wed.	Thur.	Fri.
Note:					

Also, this week they had their first self-assessment in advisory:

Name: _____   Date: _____

Class	Class Score	Effort Score	Explanation
4th Hour: Math	2	3	*I try on the homework every night, but this unit is really challenging for me and I just don't get it.*
1st Hour:			
2nd Hour:			
3rd Hour:			
4th Hour:			
5th Hour:			
6th Hour:			
7th Hour A:			
8th Hour A:			
7th Hour B:			
8th Hour B:			

Choose one class and reflect on how your effort does/does not match up with your score:

This is a **second draft**--I originally had them complete one that did not include their current "class score", which I realize was a huge mistake, because they (and I) need to be able to compare the class score with the effort score.

September -Week 4(class: 9/18): "FEELING STRESSED"

1. What is working for me: the self-evaluation is working, but I have yet to start comparing the student's self-assessment with their current academic performance (many teachers don't have too many grades in the gradebook yet, if any, so I don't have a measure for whether or not their input is equivalent to the result).
2. I did have the charts up for the first two weeks, but frankly there is not enough space anymore on my walls, and I have student work I want to display! Also, students started

Effort Chart for _____

Monday 11/3	Tuesday 11/4	Wednesday 11/5	Thursday 11/6	Friday 11/7
Monday 11/10	Tuesday 11/11	Wednesday 11/12	Thursday 11/13	Friday 11/14
Monday 11/17	Tuesday 11/18	Wednesday 11/19	Thursday 11/20	Friday 11/21
Monday 11/24	Tuesday 11/25	Wednesday 11/26	Thursday 11/27	Friday 11/28
Monday 12/1	Tuesday 12/2	Wednesday 12/3	Thursday 12/4	Friday 12/5
Monday 12/8	Tuesday 12/9	Wednesday 12/10	Thursday 12/11	Friday 12/12
Monday 12/15	Tuesday 12/16	Wednesday 12/17	Thursday 12/18	Friday 12/19

Are there any patterns that show up?

Is there one day out of the week that is consistently a high score or a lower score?

If there is a pattern that shows up, what do you think caused it?

"Great ideas originate in muscles."

*This is additional information is optional. Use at teacher's or school's discretion. They may use all or parts of this information.

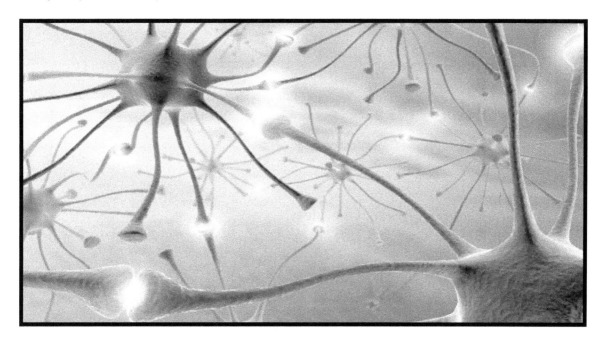

I am going to discuss how your brain works. You will have a basic understanding of your brain. You will see why we say, "Train your brain, don't let your brain train you."™

You are born with some pathways that are already stronger for you than for others. Some of us are naturally better at math, art, science, and so on. This is what Howard Gardner looked at and we have already discussed in this book.

Each time you work on one area of your learning, your brain is deepening that pathway. Each time you work on your multiplication tables, you are deepening your memory of the tables.

Depression is when your brain is not working correctly, and this is often fixed by talking to professionals about your depression. You should know that depression can happen to anyone on the planet. Depression is the brain not working correctly, and it can be fixed just like a sprained ankle. If you or a friend have lasting or reoccurring depression, please tell a trusted adult you know cares about you. They can help you get to a professional for help fixing the problem.

Write down what depression is, if it can be fixed, and if you know someone you feel has depression. When you write this down, do not use any names. Just describe the behavior that makes you think they have depression. How do we help if a friend has depression?

Write your thoughts about this topic.

Discuss as a group and record additional ideas.

Next, with your teacher, discuss as a class, and add any additional ideas to your list.

Returning to the chemicals in your brain, acetylcholine plays a big role in your learning and memory process.

Glutamate is the brain's switch for memory. When you eat a food, the switch is turned on. That is how monosodium glutamate (MSG) enhances the taste of food.

There is a lot of research that shows your brain is developing until your twenties. You do not want to do things that would stop that development. Drinking alcohol may be harmful to your brain's development if used in your teen years. That is why the law states you are to be at least twenty-one to drink. The research shows the more alcohol you drink, the more harm you do to your brain. That is true for other drugs also.

Write down your beliefs about drinking and drugs.

Discuss as a group and record additional ideas.

Discuss as a class and record any additional ideas.

My thoughts -

Just like diabetes is a chemical imbalance in the body, depression is a chemical imbalance in the brain. It can be managed with your doctor's help, prescription drugs, therapy, or group discussion or a combination of all of these.

It is very important to know this illness can be fixed with professional help. If you feel ongoing depression, find someone you trust to talk to about this. With their support, you can find a doctor who can help you!

Remember, we all deserve to be happy and healthy.

The Importance of All Citizens Voting in our Republic and Its History!

Voting is a bridge between what we would like to see our government do for us and the action the government takes. Your energy and action are a goal toward our cooperative good.

In 1776, our forefathers said they wanted to have government representation and that the English king was not giving them that. The colonists fought a war to gain this freedom. Many people died to start this country for you.

Next, we had a civil war from April 12, 1861, to May 13, 1865, so Black people could be free to choose their lives' direction. However, Black people still did not receive total freedom because many white people still believed they had a right to own slaves and that Black people were inferior to white people. It took us many generations to change that thinking for most people.

Women worked very hard to get the right to vote. It finally happened in 1920. Women are now in government, giving us different points of view about our country.

In 1965, the Voting Rights Act was enacted. It gave all Black people the right to vote. Black voting gives us even more points of view on what is best for all of us.

We have had two world wars to keep our republic in place. There are always people who want to be dictators and control others and have power over them. Many times, these people are insecure in who they are and control others to make themselves feel better. In early life, they are often bullies. In World War II, it was a man named Adolf Hitler. He had many people killed just because they were Jewish. He spread the idea of white people being superior to others. He wanted to spread this view throughout the world. In Germany, Hitler got other people to fight a war for his beliefs. In 2022, Russian leader Vladimir Putin started a war because of his belief that Ukraine is part of Russia.

The author believes the main problem with dictatorships is the isolation that dictators create. If someone disagrees with the dictator, they are killed or, many times, imprisoned. The dictator does away with the judges and law. They do not allow a difference of opinion in the news. Because of this isolation all of the weakness in the dictator's thinking and personality come into being.

Socialism is an economic and political philosophy it is characterized by social ownership as the means of production as opposed to private ownership. The problem with this system is that even though the good of the whole is considered, the system does not reward innovation for individual workers and creators. Individual creators and workers are given pay even if their work may not be at an expected level for the position the person is working at.

In our republic, we can disagree with the president and voice our views. It will take all of us to keep our republic.

My father was in World War II. He was in the navy and went to Iwo Jima to land marines. Many marines and naval personnel died fighting for your freedom.

(The author believes that cooperation is the most successful way to improve ourselves and other people around us. Just look at any sporting event or musical group. The better a team works together, the more success they have. When musicians practice and they work together, they become better at playing their instruments. The music is interesting and played better.) NATO is a great example of this, as it was formed in the 1949 to make sure we did not have another world war. It has done that. Science is another example of cooperation, as many discoveries are made with cooperation between scientists worldwide. John Lennon and Paul McCartney of the Beatles wrote many great songs together. That is why democracy works so well. Democracy depends on the imput and ideas of many people for it to work. Democracy wants works, thoughts, and ideas to rule the society, not power or might. That is way democracy has a legal system to resolve our differences. Again, please vote when you become eighteen as your voice is important.

Please honor all the past people who fought and died so that you can vote.

Please, when you become age eighteen, please vote to keep this republic alive and well!

Your opinions and ideas matter to the health of this country!

Remember that effort will also equate to more success, that you can do anything if you work hard enough and long enough on it!

Sometimes the work will take years to complete!

My wish for you is joy and happiness!
Remember if you are not successful in some area of life, it is a lesson, not a failure!

Thank you for reading and learning from my book!

Acknowledgments

I want to say thank you to my loving and nurturing parents, Richard and Bunny Jones. They helped me see what good loving energy and hard work does to make people's lives better. Thanks to Nanette and Jennifer, my siblings, for growing up with me.

I am thankful for the community of Morgan Park in Duluth, Minnesota, where we enjoyed a community center built by US Steel that had a pool, bowling lanes, a running track, a basketball court, a handball room, pool tables, table tennis, a boxing ring, an auditorium, a tennis court, and meeting rooms for Boy Scouts and other organizations.

Thank you to the many teachers and coaches who helped me be successful in my education and in sports—Dick Forbort, Rolly Strand, Soup Stromme, Miles Vukson, Quentin Junger, and Don Derbishire. Special thanks to my dear track and cross-country coach, Paul Nace, for all the support he offered to help me become a top performer in the state.

Thank you to my beautiful, kind, and loving Partner in Life, Jo Jo Peterson. She gives me inspiration and joy each and every day.

I'm grateful for my educational experiences at Minnesota State University–Mankato (bachelor of science), at Saint Mary's University of Minnesota(master's), and through the University of Minnesota's enrichment support led by Professor Tom Post. Thank you to the National Science Foundation (NSF) and to Ed Anderson, who wrote the five-year grant program, Open Access, that offered me a .4 position with the NSF program (looking at the new math curriculum that came out in the mid-1990s). Minneapolis School System, led by my math chairmanship, chose the Connected Mathematics Project (CMP) math that is still being used today.

Thank you to the principals who supported my efforts to be an educational leader and encouraged me to help my students to be successful in their learning, even when my strategies opposed the status quo: Harold Kergassler, Owatonna, Minnesota; Bob Lariccia, Warrensville Heights, Ohio; and John Googgins, Shannon Griffen, and Donna Amann, Minneapolis, Minnesota.

A very special thank-you to Bernadeia Johnson, a former superintendent of Minneapolis Public Schools, for believing in me enough to ask me to be part of the Minneapolis Think Tank, and to Father Jewison of St. John Vianney School in Fairmont, Minnesota, for giving me my start in creating new educational ideas with an after-school program for high school students.

My gratitude to the students and programs that helped me grow as a person, educator, and coach—Fairmont Schools, St. John Vianney School, Owatonna Schools, Warrensville Heights Junior High, Randolph School, Minneapolis Public Schools, and especially the Minneapolis Federation of Teachers for their support in testing this program through Quality Compensation (Q Comp) funding. A special thanks to Paul Hegre, Emily Olson, Rachel Gore, Emily Maxwell, Maggie Sullivan, and Lynn Nordgren for the opportunity to improve this program through a research-based process.

Thank you to all the Minneapolis teachers who took the Education2Aspire course and asked me to write this book. And, of course, thank you to Rod Martel for the acronym ASPIRE.

About Education2Aspire

Education2Aspire is a nonprofit company working with educators and school systems to help their students succeed in their learning. You can give your financial support by going to our website and contributing to this important work.

For more information about how Education2Aspire can help your school systems, educators, and support staff through our professional development workshops and seminars, contact us at (952) 270-9417 or www.Education2Aspire.com.

Resources

Here are some resources that have helped me formulate my ideas over the years. Perhaps you'll find them useful as well.

Connellan, Thomas. *Bringing Out the Best in Others.* Bard Press, 2003.

Glasser, William. *Control Theory: A New Explanation of How We Control Our Lives.* New York: Harper & Row Publishers, 1985.

———. *The Quality School: Managing Students without Coercion.* New York: HarperCollins, 1990.

———. *Reality Therapy: A New Approach to Psychiatry.* New York: Harper & Row Publishers, Inc., 1965.

Gossen, Diane C. *Restitution: Restructuring School Discipline.* Chapel Hill, NC: New View Publications, 1996.

Kohn, Alfie. *Punished by Rewards: The Trouble with Gold Stars, Incentive Plans, A's, Praise, and Other Bribes.* Boston: Houghton Mifflin Company, 1993.

Printed in the USA
CPSIA information can be obtained
at www.ICGtesting.com
LVHW082334210924
791601LV00003B/18